DIARY OF A MAD JUROR

An Inside Look at a Record-Breaking Wrongful-Death Trial that Fell Short of the Truth

CYNTHIA M. PIGOTT

Published by:
Scout's Press
NEW YORK, NY
MADJURORDIARY@GMAIL.COM

ISBN-13: 978-0-578-94661-0

Cover and interior by Gary A. Rosenberg
www.thebookcouple.com

Printed in the United States of America

For my husband, Bob,
my favorite lawyer

*"The truth is rarely pure
and never simple."*

—Oscar Wilde,
The Importance of Being Earnest

CONTENTS

The Diary, Part Two

DIARY OF A MAD JUROR

THE ACCIDENT
(May 2008)

On May 30, 2008, thirty-year-old Don Leo crawled out of bed at four-thirty in the morning, grabbed breakfast, planted a see-ya-later kiss on his sleeping fiancée, and climbed behind the wheel of his beat-up Honda Accord. A workhorse that got him the seventy or so miles from his Jersey-shore home to his current gig, operating a crane on a construction site in Manhattan.

* * *

Twenty-eight-year-old Ramadan Kurtaj (pronounced kurt-EYE), an Eastern European immigrant, had it easier: He woke up in his Bronx apartment after the sun rose, and caught a ride to today's job, digging sewers under a new high-rise.

Between slurps of coffee, Ramadan asked his coworker, "Where are we headed this time?"

"Upper East Side," he replied, weaving his way through southbound traffic on the FDR Drive.

* * *

At a few minutes before eight, Devorah Zamansky deposited her son at school, then drove north to her job as an assistant principal in Upper Manhattan. As she approached the northwest corner of Ninety-First Street and First Avenue, a meteor-like object hurtled toward her car. Devorah swerved to her right, pulled through the intersection, and stopped after half a block. When she turned around, she saw a studio apartment–sized piece of machinery embedded in the asphalt just inches behind her. Shaken and teary, Devorah called her husband to report her narrow escape.

* * *

Don and Ramadan hadn't been so lucky. The plunging object was a crane operator's cab, which had suddenly split off the top of its two hundred feet–high tower. Don, who was trapped inside, was found dead on impact. The seventy-five-ton behemoth landed on top of Ramadan, who succumbed to his injuries at a local hospital some three hours later.

* * *

It had been a split-second accident, but it would take endless legal proceedings, over a period of ten years, for justice to be served.

* * *

When the case was over, a juror on the civil trial—at eleven months, the longest ever held in Manhattan—looked for answers to questions that had dogged her throughout. Months of sleuthing led her to an unsettling conclusion: The courtroom is *not* the place to look for the truth.

The Diary, Part One

THE TRIAL
(September 2014–
August 2015)

ONE

JURY SELECTION

September 3, 2014

I was about to toss the letter in the junk-mail pile when I noticed its telltale gothic script.

"You are summoned to serve as a juror in New York County Supreme Court at Sixty Centre Street at 8:30 a.m. on Tuesday, September 16, 2014," it read.

Having exhausted my allotted number of stay-at-home-mom child-care postponements, I knew I'd have to show up this time.

September 16

When I emerged from the City Hall subway stop deep beneath downtown Manhattan, Foley Square's expanse of government buildings enveloped me. Why is it that so many squares in New York City aren't square? I wondered as I searched for the correct courthouse. At last, I spied a long, slow-moving line of would-be jurors snaking up Sixty Centre Street's broad flight of stairs, made famous by the TV show *Law & Order*.

Once inside, we passed through security, many of us handing our precious takeout cups of coffee to the guards so they wouldn't get zapped by the x-ray machine. Then we entered the grand rotunda and shoved our way onto an elevator to Room 452. We passed by an old wooden booth sans pay phone, plus rows of benches filled mostly by pallid men wearing ill-fitting suits and clutching banged-up briefcases. Lawyers, I presumed. They kept their heads down, ignoring the parade that would decide their clients' fates.

A jury clerk atop an old wooden dais (what is it with all the old wood in this place?) leaned down to hand me a questionnaire in exchange for my summons.

What would the Court care to know about me, I wondered?

Standard personal information—in a senior moment (or a moment of denial), I answered "fifty-three" instead of "fifty-four" to the question about my age, and had to ask for the form back when I realized my mistake. The Court wanted to know that I was born in Detroit, Michigan, and that I'd lived in New York City for almost thirty years, but it didn't care where I'd been in between.

The questionnaire, I realized, skipped the most exceptional part of my life: the eight years I lived with my parents in London, England, from ages nine to seventeen. Never mind. My semi-British upbringing would likely be of no consequence in a New York City courtroom.

Next the Court wanted to know if I am, or if anyone in my family is, an attorney. After deciding that my cousin

Bryan was too distant a relative, I listed my husband, Bob, only.

Had I served on a jury before? I'd almost forgotten that criminal trial on which I'd served in the early nineteen nineties, when I'd been sequestered in a hotel room for a night.

Had I been the victim of a crime? I'll *never* forget the time I was mugged soon after I moved to New York back in the eighties.

The rest of the questions—whether I've been accused or convicted of committing a crime, been a witness in court, or been involved in a lawsuit—I was glad to answer in the negative.

The Court also didn't care what I'd done before I became a mom. Wouldn't they like to know that I'd been a reporter/writer/editor for a decade, which means I'm one of those question-everything types a trial lawyer might want to steer clear of?

* * *

Once the stragglers had finished their surveys, we were treated to a film about jury duty called *Your Turn*. My turn for what? "A firsthand look at, and a chance to make a mark on, the justice system," the narrator proclaimed solemnly.

I considered the title's promise. Did I have time to take a turn? Yes. My stay-at-home-mom responsibilities are virtually nil, now that James is in his first year of college, and Jules is in tenth grade.

Did I want a turn? My previous stint as a juror had been discouraging. I'd been the last holdout for a guilty vote, and I'd caved so that the jury wouldn't be sequestered for a second night.

My "mark on the law" had been shameful, and my "firsthand look at the justice system" had been gloomy.

But I'd like to give jury duty another chance. If chosen, I promised myself, this time my "mark" would be noble. If chosen, my "firsthand look" would be uplifting.

September 17

I was glued to my book, *Wild* by Cheryl Strayed, while waiting in the jurors' "holding pen" this morning. The author had bravely abandoned her old life so she could hike the Pacific Crest Trail, solo no less. Was my choice in reading material telling me something? If the author could take a hiatus, so could I.

"Cynthia Pee-JEAU?" Silence. "Cynthia PIE-gought?"

Wait . . . that was *my* name the clerk was calling. Typical. "It's pronounced PIG-it," I felt like correcting her, but didn't, not wanting to seem snippy.

I joined a group headed for Room 300 to undergo *voir dire* (literally, "to speak the truth"), the process by which lawyers question potential jurors. The few seats in the hallway outside our new abode were taken, so I joined the standing majority, all sixty or seventy of us milling around like cattle waiting to be herded. As a court officer took attendance, the herd gathered toward its next destination, an actual courtroom.

My name was never announced. I approached the court officer warily.

"You didn't call me," I said, giving her my name.

"You're not on my list," she scowled. "Wait here." She stomped off, then returned a few minutes later. "Go ahead and join the others," she commanded, heaving a sigh.

* * *

Once inside, we wannabe (and don't wannabe) jurors were closely observed by a judge and a frighteningly long row of lawyers. "I wasn't expecting the 'Spanish Inquisition'," I whispered to my seatmate, who stifled a laugh.

His Honor gave us an overview of the matter at hand, a "wrongful-death" civil trial in which twelve jurors—six regulars and six alternates—will hear evidence regarding liability and damages (monetary compensation).

In 2008, the judge continued, a tower crane collapsed on Manhattan's Upper East Side, killing two construction workers, Donald Christopher Leo, a native New Yorker, and Ramadan Kurtaj, an immigrant from Eastern Europe.

Hold on, this sounds familiar, I thought. As his Honor provided more information, it dawned on me: The judge was describing an accident that happened just three blocks from my home six years ago. It was a disappointing coincidence. When the lawyers find out that I live nearby, I'll probably be eliminated.

At the end of his overview, the judge warned us that the trial was expected to last three months. Whoa! If by some chance I *were* chosen, that would be one long hiatus. Did I still want it?

When I reflected on my daily routine, made up of my kids' (waning) needs, household chores, hobbies, trips to the gym, and the occasional coffee klatch, I thought: If called to serve, I can afford to take three months off. I can afford to say yes.

September 18

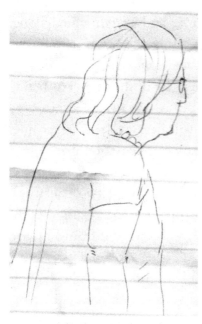

Susan Karten, a lawyer for the Kurtaj estate.
Courtroom Sketch by Juror Alison Colby.

A diminutive attorney with dyed blond hair approached me in the late afternoon. My heart beat faster.

"I see from your questionnaire that your husband is an attorney," commented Susan Karten, a sixty-something white woman with a tinny voice. "What type of law does he practice?"

"He's the general counsel for a nonprofit that develops affordable housing," I replied.

"Do you ever use your degree in French Literature?"

"Not really."

I'd detected a note of snideness behind her question about my admittedly impractical college major, and decided I wasn't crazy about this lady.

My inquisitor was about to move on to the next candidate when I interjected, "I have to tell you something: I live near the accident site, and I saw the wreckage." She didn't bat an eye, and I liked her better. Maybe I *was* still in the running.

After the last juror was questioned, the judge and the lawyers left us alone with the ever-officious court officer, a tall Black woman who never cracks a smile. Upon their return, the attorneys asked those who had made the first cut to move, one group at a time, to the jury box. Individual candidates disappeared through a back door that led who knows where; they returned stone-faced to their original seats a few minutes later.

I was surprised when my number was called, and moved to the front gingerly. When it was my turn, I followed a dark hallway to a tiny room on my left, where the lawyers were squeezed next to one another at a rectangular table headed by the judge.

He peered at me as I faced him self-consciously.

"Is there any reason you can't serve on this trial?" the judge intoned.

"No, sir," I replied, then added, so as not to seem like a patsy, "Guess *that* was the wrong answer." He and the lawyers chuckled knowingly.

When the names of the final twelve were called, mine was among them.

The trial starts in two weeks.

TWO

OPENING STATEMENTS

October 2

W hen I told my lawyer husband that I'd been selected as a juror, he wasn't surprised. "You're just the type we look for," Bob declared. "Pleasant demeanor. Not a rabble rouser."

"Gee, thanks," I replied. "You make me sound like milquetoast."

"Don't worry," Bob assured me. "*I* know there's more to you than meets the eye."

* * *

We "chosen" ones glanced at one another with suspicion outside the courtroom this morning. Supposedly, we were a jury of peers, but we seemed a motley crew. Eight women and four men; seven whites, three Blacks, and two Hispanics; the youngest, twenty-something, and the oldest, sixty-something. Yet each of us had been deemed suitable to serve, and each of us was willing, so we must have *something* in common. Time—of which we will have plenty—will tell.

* * *

The same court officer who had managed us during *voir dire* marched toward us determinedly, then lined us up in numbered order. (I'm Alternate Number Four.) I felt like I was about to be judged, not the other way around, and my heart once again beat faster. We shuffled down a narrow hallway, then turned left past the same room where we'd told the "Spanish Inquisition" that we were down with a three-month commitment.

Melanie, our leader's incongruously sunny-sounding name, reached for a handkerchief to pat a recurring sheen of sweat off her forehead. She peeked through a crack in the courtroom door, then delivered the "All rise" command. I was awed by the silent standing ovation.

"You may be seated," declared the judge, the Honorary Manuel J. Mendez, addressing the lawyers and the attendees in the gallery. "The jurors please remain standing."

A clerk asked each lawyer to confirm that the jury was acceptable, and then we took the jury oath en masse, pledging to act "fairly and impartially," and to "follow the law as it is explained to us by the judge." This new world still didn't seem real. It felt like we were actors in a courtroom drama, that soon the director would yell "Cut!" But when the judge was interrupted by a blast of music from a rally in Foley Square, it was clear this wasn't make-believe.

"It's just our luck that right when we start the trial, there's a party outside," Mendez shouted with a grudging laugh.

Judge Manuel J. Mendez. *Courtroom Sketch by Juror Alison Colby.*

After we sat down, the judge reintroduced the lawyers. There were six on the plaintiffs' side—three for the estate of Donald Christopher Leo, and three for the estate of Ramadan Kurtaj—and ten for the defendants, including the owner of the collapsed crane, James F. Lomma (pronounced LOW-ma). We were outnumbered: sixteen lawyers versus twelve jurors.

The fifty-something Hispanic judge, of average height and build, smiled at us encouragingly as he explained how the trial would proceed. "First the lawyers will give opening statements," he said, "when they outline their respective cases." I remembered my husband once meticulously preparing an opening statement when one of his cases went

13

to trial. "It's an important opportunity to make a good first impression on the jury," he'd told me. "It's also a rare chance to speak without being interrupted by the opposing attorneys."

Mendez was cut off by the sing-song ring of a cell phone, and dirty looks abounded until its owner, Alternate Number One, silenced it. The judge cleared his throat, then continued. "Next the lawyers will present evidence," he explained, in the form of testimony, documents, photos, etcetera. After the attorneys' closing summaries, he concluded, six jurors will deliberate and deliver a verdict.

"There is no magic formula by which you will evaluate testimony," Mendez told us. "You bring with you into this courtroom all the experience and background of your lives. In your everyday affairs, you decide for yourselves the reliability or unreliability of the things people tell you. The same tests that you use in your everyday dealings are the tests you should apply here." Sounded like a piece of cake.

At the end, the judge delivered a couple of warnings.

One: "If you see any of the parties involved in this case outside the courtroom, ignore them. They have all been ordered to do the same. In no other way can they be assured of absolute impartiality." No smiles, no good mornings, no acknowledgments whatsoever. It was a peculiarly unfriendly society we jurors were joining.

Two: "Do not discuss this case among yourselves—"Great, I thought, we can't talk about the *one* thing we have in common (so far)—"or with anyone else. Do not do an internet search about this case. Do not read newspaper reports, listen to radio reports, or watch television reports about this case. Do not let anyone who has read, heard, or seen such reports tell you about them."

In other words, don't let anything break through this new world's hermetic seal.

October 3

As I squeezed onto a subway car along with an army of commuters this morning, I thought proudly, "I'm one of you again." Okay, I'm not going to work per se; but I do have a "job." It felt good to have a purpose beyond hearth and home.

"Hi, Cynthia!" a voice in the throng bellowed.

It came from the mother of one of my daughter's classmates, a woman with a legitimate, high-powered career. When I told her that I was on my way to jury duty, she shot me a look of pity. "Poor you," she declared. I was determined *not* to let her offhand remark burst my bubble.

* * *

Back in the courtroom, Bernadette Panzella, a lawyer for the Leo estate, began her opening statement. "Instead of dancing at the wedding of their firstborn child, his parents were burying him," she declared solemnly.

Panzella had explained that Donald (Don) Christopher Leo, the thirty-year-old operator of the crane, was killed just three weeks before he was to be married. To drive this tragic turn of events home, she introduced the wedding invitation into evidence.

Don was a regular, stand-up guy who was born and raised in the borough of Staten Island, Panzella told us. After introducing the jury to Don's mother, Maria, a pleasant-looking woman in the front row of the gallery, Panzella set up a poster-sized photo of the deceased—brown hair and eyes, wide smile, handsome if plumpish face—just inches in front of the jury box.

One of the defense attorneys grumbled,

Deceased plaintiff Donald Christopher Leo.
Courtroom Sketch by Juror Alison Colby.

"Judge, it's blocking my view of the jurors."

"Ms. Panzella, please push it back a little," Mendez told her.

"Of course, your Honor," she replied deferentially, but nudged the poster so slightly that the complainer still couldn't see around it. He glared at her.

* * *

Before this trial, I'd had two notions of the typical personal-injury lawyer. One was the scruffy ambulance chaser; the other was the slick, "I can get you—and me—a pot of money" advocate you see in those late-night TV ads. Panzella would fit perfectly in the latter group, I thought, if she weren't female.

I guess most women are turned off by the unseemliness of this specialization. Not Panzella. A tall white woman "of a certain age" who was dressed and coiffed to a T, she had begun her opening with the following: "I have a big mouth, and I can project despite the noise from the rally outside." Her gesticulations, which were punctuated

Bernadette Panzella,
a lawyer for the Leo estate.
*Courtroom Sketch by
Juror Alison Colby.*

by a jangly assortment of bracelets on both wrists, were as outsized as her voice.

To say that Panzella's opening statement was hard to follow would be an understatement: She jumped back and forth between topics in a dizzying fashion. She also repeated herself mercilessly. At one point, she acknowledged, "I know, you're probably sick of hearing this," alluding to the malignant character of Lomma, the crane owner.

Nevertheless, I managed to ascertain the crux of Panzella's argument. Don Leo didn't cause the accident. Who did? The crane owner and the rest of the defendants, including the developers, the contractors, and the owner of the land where a condominium and a school were being constructed.

October 6

Michael O'Neill delivered the opening statement for the other plaintiff, the estate of Ramadan Kurtaj, a sewer worker from the Eastern European country of Kosovo who died after the crane's cab landed on top of him.

This late-fifties attorney, with straight, salt-and-pepper hair atop a Harrison Ford–ish face, concurred that the crane operator did not cause the accident. He claimed that Lomma (the crane owner) and the concrete sub-contractor, a company called Sorbara, actually knew that the crane was dangerous—and that the other defendants should have known.

"Even though the crane had a mechanical defect," O'Neill argued, "the defendants put it to work anyway, because it was fast—powered by diesel fuel, it ran more quickly than the more common electric tower crane—and because

Michael O'Neill, a lawyer for the Kurtaj estate.
Courtroom Sketch by Juror Alison Colby.

it was available." (Due to a building boom, tower cranes were in great demand in New York City in 2008.)

"In the construction business, time is money," claimed O'Neill, whose nasal—possibly Midwestern—speech, and preppy attire, distinguished him from the other attorneys. "The evidence will paint a picture of an ugly culture in this industry. Do whatever it takes to keep the job going. Don't bother with safety, if it's going to slow work down."

October 9

This morning, I sat next to Juror Number Three, a pretty Hispanic woman with wide-set eyes and full lips, while we waited in a back hallway that serves as our jury's waiting room.

"My name's Aisha," she introduced herself.

"I'm Cynthia. I'm curious, were you named for Stevie Wonder's baby in the song 'Isn't She Lovely'?" I asked.

Aisha raised her immaculately plucked eyebrows, as if surprised by my familiarity with Mr. Wonder's work. "Yes," she replied. "My mom *loved* that song."

My question was an effective icebreaker. A stock clerk in a clothing store, Aisha told me she's the single mother of two girls and two boys, and she showed me their photos on her cell phone. "My oldest is twenty," she mentioned. How is that possible? I wondered. Aisha looks too young to have a twenty-year-old. (Later I found out that she's thirty-six, the same age I was when I gave birth to my first child.)

"Did you have a good day off?" I asked. (We don't come to court on Wednesdays, when Judge Mendez attends to other cases on his docket.)

"Yeah. I spent the evening lying in bed with my kids watching videos," she replied.

I'm ashamed to admit it: As a middle-class mom in a stable marriage, I'd felt sorry for Aisha at the start of our conversation. But this answer brought me down a peg or two. I wished I had that kind of intimate connection with my standoffish children.

* * *

The defense introduced their side of the story today. First up was Glenn Fuerth, who represents Lomma, the crane owner, as well as two of his businesses, New York Crane, Inc., and J.F. Lomma, Inc. Too bad he doesn't look like Colin Firth, I thought when I heard his surname and incorrectly assumed it was spelled the same way as that of the devilishly handsome British actor. Bald, save a few gray wisps that hung from his creamy pate, Fuerth wore round, wire-rimmed glasses and a baggy suit over his skinny frame.

Glenn Fuerth, a lawyer for defendant Lomma.
Courtroom Sketch by Juror Alison Colby.

He began by attempting to paint a sympathetic portrait of his client, big businessperson number one in this case. Just like Don Leo, Fuerth told us, Lomma started out as a blue-collar worker. But by the nineteen nineties, this self-made man had formed the first of his many companies, including New York Crane, which owned the machine at issue in this case.

Lomma, whose "empire" now includes some twenty businesses, exemplifies, according to his lawyer, the Great American Success Story. "I don't think there's anything wrong with getting ahead and making money," Fuerth said in a monotone voice, countering the plaintiffs' attorneys' contention that Lomma is a wheeler-dealer.

Fuerth claimed it was not a mechanical defect, but improper operation of the crane that caused the collapse. Yikes, I thought: Fuerth must have known that he was treading on thin ice by blaming one of the victims, Don Leo, the crane operator who's no longer around to defend himself. He'd better have some solid evidence up his sleeve to make this a winning strategy.

Fuerth wrapped up by claiming that the plaintiffs' lawyers had obfuscated the truth in their openings. "I was reminded of a quote from Shakespeare: 'Oh, what a tangled web we weave, when we intend to deceive.'" He was right that Panzella's disorganized opening had been a "tangled web," but whether her intention was to deceive remained to be seen. In any case, Juror Number Five (whose name I still don't know) told me afterwards that Fuerth got it wrong: Sir Walter Scott made this observation, not Shakespeare.

* * *

On the way home, I realized that Fuerth's case was a tough sell from the get-go. Why? Because most human beings (jurors included), no matter their personalities or backgrounds, are hardwired to root for the little guy, for the David in any David and Goliath–themed story. And despite Lomma's humble beginnings, he's not the David in the story behind this trial. Don and Ramadan are the Davids.

Given this scenario, I thought, it's going to be really hard to uphold the oath I took on day one of the trial: to be a "fair and impartial" juror.

October 10

Here was the essence of the opening statements delivered by the lawyers for the owner of the land, plus the developers of and general contractor for the project where the tragedy occurred: We didn't have anything to do with renting the crane or hiring its operator, so we weren't negligent, no matter which theory of the accident you believe.

It seemed a supremely reasonable argument, I thought, resisting my anti-Goliath bias tooth and nail.

* * *

During a break, I sat next to a slender, shaggy-haired white man who sported oversized spectacles, an expensive-looking leather jacket, and mismatched patterned socks. Alternate Number Three had the look of an aging (approaching sixty?) rocker, a la Keith Richards, but without the hard-living edges.

"Hi, my name's Guy," he said, extending his hand.

I was a little intimidated by this juror's hip demeanor, but we bridged the gap.

"What do you do when you're not at Sixty Centre Street?" I asked.

"Well, I'm married, and I'm a dad. I have two girls, aged nine and seven."

After I told him about my kids, Guy added matter-of-factly that he's the chief technology officer of a division of a world-famous company. How could someone with such a prominent job devote three months to jury duty? I wondered. Perhaps he's one of those executives who's so high on the totem pole that he can do whatever he likes.

October 13

"I'm trying to imagine what it's like to be you," Ray Slattery, who represents Sorbara, the concrete supplier that rented the crane from Lomma, told the jury this morning. "You hear one party give their opening, and you're swayed one way, and you hear another party give their opening, and you're swayed another way." Slattery's job was to sway us his way and keep us there.

Slattery seemed a jovial sort, with a shock of white hair, an ample belly, and a gleam in his eye. (Yes, I *am* aware that I'm describing the archetypal Santa Claus, which isn't a bad look for a trial attorney.)

Before he continued his statement, Slattery introduced us to the husband-and-wife team, Marino and Carmela Sorbara, who head their namesake company. Sitting on the defendants' side of the audience, they were humbly dressed, holding hands and smiling nervously at each other, as well as the jury. They're mom-and-pop types, not corporate Goliaths, so it shouldn't be hard for me to judge them fairly, I reasoned.

Despite his clients' pleasing demeanor, Slattery had his work cut out for him. He was the only lawyer in this trial who had to disprove *both* theories of the accident's cause—mechanical failure *and* operator error—to protect his client. This was because the Sorbara company was at least partly responsible for the crane, which it had rented from Lomma, *and* for its operator, which it had hired from the local crane operators' union.

Ray Slattery, a lawyer for defendant Sorbara.
Courtroom Sketch by Juror Alison Colby.

This was the gist of Slattery's defense: "Sorbara had used this same crane on its previous job, when a mechanical problem was found," he freely admitted. "But my client assumed New York Crane had fixed it and made it safe for the next job, the one on Ninety-First Street. If the repair wasn't done properly," Slattery continued, "Sorbara didn't know, and it wouldn't have rented the crane if it had."

What's more, Sorbara hired a solid crane operator. "No one saw Don do anything dangerous on the morning of the accident, or on any other day," Slattery declared unequivocally. "Besides, why would Don do something that might put his own life in danger?"

Slattery's arguments made perfect sense to me.

* * *

This afternoon I had lunch with Juror Number Two, Aaron, and Number Six, Tony. We ended up at a health-food restaurant for fitness enthusiasts, which both of them are. I, on the other hand, am about as toned as cooked spaghetti (despite frequent gym visits). But my turkey chili bowl was surprisingly tasty, and I polished it off like someone loading up for a triathlon. The guys seemed impressed: I got the feeling the women they usually eat with are the type who claim to be full after a few bites.

To my surprise, both Tony and Aaron are police officers. I'd have thought that cops, like attorneys, would rarely—if ever—be chosen as jurors, since they might be too familiar with the law to be objective. Maybe the defense lawyers took a chance on them because they thought that cops, who are supposed to be tough, straight-arrow types, would be less likely to be swayed by the plaintiffs' tales of woe.

In any case, it turned out that Tony had been one of Aaron's instructors at the police academy, so they'd actually met before the trial. Tony, a fortyish, nearly bald white man with grey-green eyes, an aquiline nose, and an open posture, works in central booking ("where new arrests are processed," he explained when I gave him a puzzled look) at a criminal court in an outer borough. Aaron, who looks to be in his thirties, is in the NYPD's narcotics division, which means he chases down drug dealers for a living.

"I made an arrest Wednesday night [he and Tony work on our day off from jury duty], and the guy had *really* nice wood floors in his apartment," Aaron told me.

That was *not* how I'd expected this tall, muscular, light-skinned Black police officer to describe his night of crime-fighting.

"Look," Aaron added. "I took a picture on my phone. I want to get this kind of flooring for my new house." I expressed my approval while wondering if it was kosher to use a crime-scene photo for home improvement purposes.

I was determined to make the most of this rare opportunity to chat with police officers. (Before this, my only exchanges with cops had been to ask for directions or to weasel my way out of a traffic violation.)

"So, Aaron, why did you become a police officer?" I asked bluntly.

"Well, right after the September eleven terrorist attack, I was riding the subway to my IT job, where I sat in a cubicle all day long, and I thought, I can't do this anymore. This isn't me. I need to feel like I'm contributing somehow." He added that his parents had also worked for the City—his father was a corrections officer, and his mother was an education department administrator.

"I come from a family of civil servants, too," Tony chimed in. "My dad was a City bus driver, and my mom was a high-school guidance counselor. I have a sister who was a parole officer, and another who's a retired police officer." Tony paused, then added, "I like helping people, and public service is the right fit for me. Anyway, I never cared much about making money."

While we returned to the courthouse, I thought: If I was right that the defense chose Tony and Aaron because they expected them to be hard-hearted rule followers, they may be disappointed. What's more, Tony's disdain for money suggested he might not be impressed by a bunch of big-business defendants, particularly Lomma, the crane owner.

* * *

On the subway ride home, I had another realization, this one personal in nature. My lunch with Tony and Aaron—like my conversation with Aisha—had taken me out of my social bubble. Unlike Tony and Aaron, my "real-world" friends (yes, I was already starting to think of the jurors as friends) are not particularly altruistic. Sure, some of them have dabbled in contributing to society: stints in the Peace Corps, first jobs as underpaid teachers, and the odd volunteer gig. But none have made a career of it. Instead, they've devoted their lives to personal gain.

And even though I'd sacrificed a career I loved to become a stay-at-home mother, which I've always considered a selfless act, my choice helped my family, not my fellow man.

October 14

When I got to our hallway-cum-jury room this morning, Tony and Aaron had started a poker game with Juror Number Five, whose name is Martha. In her late sixties, Martha is, I believe, the oldest member of our group. A tall, white woman with wavy brown hair, she's always well put together (a flowing blouse, pressed trousers, and ballet flats are a preferred outfit).

"What do you do for a living?" I overheard Tony ask Martha.

"I'm a retired therapist. I'm also an abstract artist. But I haven't had much time to work lately," she added with a frown.

"I'm an amateur painter myself," I interjected," but I haven't done any painting since the trial started, either."

No big deal, I thought: Martha and I will be able to pick up our brushes again by New Year's.

* * *

Why would a shipping company be embroiled in this trial? I wondered when Robert Fumo, the thirty-something lawyer for the last defendant, Brady Marine, took the podium. Granted, the plaintiffs have thrown everything but the kitchen sink at this case, but there has to be *some* limit to their reach.

"Brady Marine's primary business is, indeed, the repair of ships," this soft-spoken, remarkably pale attorney told us. (The mother in me wanted to admonish Fumo to eat his spinach.) "However, my client also fixes metal machinery, including cranes."

At this juncture, Fumo introduced us to Brady Marine's president, Daniel Muirhead, who was in attendance today. It was a smart move, because Muirhead, like the Sorbaras, looked the part of the congenial small-business owner.

"You've heard that one theory of the accident's cause is that the crane had a defect [a faulty weld in its bearing, the part that houses the turntable, which allows the crane to pivot]," Fumo continued. "My client *did* do some welding on the crane, but Brady Marine did *not* manufacture the weld that allegedly snapped." The welding Brady did remained intact, even after the accident, according to

Robert Fumo, a lawyer for defendant Brady Marine. *Courtroom Sketch by Juror Alison Colby.*

Fumo. "Therefore there was no negligence on the part of my client," he stated earnestly.

Like Slattery before him, Fumo's argument made sense, and he and his affable client were easy to take at face value.

THREE

THE PLAINTIFFS' CASE: LIABILITY

October 16

In the courtroom this morning, Panzella, the lead attorney for the Leo estate, began her case by playing a recording of frantic nine-one-one calls placed at the time of the accident. "Something came crashing to the ground . . . at Ninety-First and First . . . I hear screaming . . . please, come quick." It was a great way to reel us in: We jurors leaned forward in unison, like sports fans during match point, to discern each anguished plea for help. Panzella remained uncharacteristically silent throughout.

Before our first live witness testified, Melanie, our court officer, handed each of us a notebook. "Because this trial will be complex," Judge Mendez explained, "the Court will allow you to take notes." Uh-oh, I thought: I hope I can handle "complex."

* * *

Panzella's first order of business was to prove that her client, Don Leo, did *not* cause the accident. To this end, she called to the stand a fiftyish crane operator named John Samuels, who had been Don's colleague on the Ninety-First Street job. Samuels seemed uncomfortable in the suit that loosely covered his lanky frame, and his collared shirt was tie-less. As he shifted in his seat and peered at us jurors warily, I suddenly questioned my ability to judge him. What right did I—a stay-at-home mom/former editor—have to evaluate his testimony? I know nothing of his world.

In olden times, jurors were chosen specifically because they were familiar with the case at hand, which seems eminently sensible. Nowadays, however, such knowledge is considered a prejudicial liability. A blank-slate, common-sense approach is deemed the fairest. I guess I'm as level-headed as the next guy, so I hunkered down and played the role I'd agreed to fulfill.

"I was actually supposed to be in the crane cab on the morning of May thirtieth," Samuels told Panzella with a shudder. "But Don had an afternoon appointment with the priest who was going to perform his wedding, so he asked if I'd switch shifts.

"I was having breakfast at a diner just a block away when the crane came down," Samuels continued. "I don't know how I didn't hear it. When I came out, I looked up the street, and the crane had disappeared. I pushed my way through the crowd to get closer, and I couldn't believe my eyes.

"I called Don's father, who was also a crane operator and had filled in for Don at Ninety-First Street when Don took a bachelor-party trip." Samuels paused. "Don's father arrived a few minutes later." Don was lying on a gurney, and his father fell to his knees, draped his body over his son, and wept.

"Let's take a break," said Judge Mendez. The jury filed out somberly.

"That was moving," said Guy.

"Yeah. Poor Don," Tony replied.

You'd have to be made of stone not to agree, I thought. Then I pinched myself. Remember, Cynthia: Don't let sympathy color your judgment.

* * *

Back in the courtroom, Panzella asked Samuels, "What was your opinion of Don's ability as a crane operator?"

"I was impressed by his skills," he replied. "For a young guy, he had a lot of poise, and he controlled the crane well."

I christened my notebook with the following: "I wonder what Samuels meant by 'for a young guy' when he described Don Leo? Was he suggesting he lacked experience? And will the defense make hay of this offhand remark?"

October 17

I faced my first test of my new world's peculiar social conventions in the unlikeliest of places this morning: the ladies' room.

Don Leo's mother and Panzella were ahead of me in line; to avoid making rule-breaking eye contact, I stared at a discolored blotch on the wall that became a judge's gavel in my imagination. When we three entered adjacent stalls, I hummed "Happy" by Pharrell Williams in my head until I heard them exit. Then I ended up between Mrs. Leo and her lawyer at the long row of sinks, so I rinsed my hands of every single speck of soap, waiting until they'd cleared the scene. This no-contact with the parties/lawyers/witnesses commandment may drive me to distraction, I thought.

* * *

In the courtroom, Samuels, Don Leo's crane-operator partner, returned to the stand. He explained that all cranes have safety switches, whose purpose is to sound warning alarms and prevent accidents like the one at Ninety-First Street.

"We test these devices every single morning before we start work," Samuels assured us. "They were checked on the morning of the accident, and they were working properly." This meant his friend Don *couldn't* have caused the accident, even if he'd tried.

I had no reason to disbelieve Samuels: After all, these workers' own livelihoods—and lives—were on the line.

* * *

Fuerth was the first defense attorney to cross-examine Samuels, on behalf of Lomma, the crane owner. Fuerth's objective was to prove, through this witness's testimony, that Don Leo *did* cause the accident.

To my surprise, Fuerth did not run with Samuels's

comment regarding Leo's relative youth and lack of experience. Rather, Fuerth blamed the safety switches, which, he claimed, were *not,* in fact, functioning on the day of the accident. Because these devices had been disengaged, according to Fuerth, Don Leo was able to raise both the boom and the hoist line too high, unsafe maneuvers that destabilized the crane, broke the bearing's weld, and caused the crane to collapse.

"You had to disable the safety switches in order to make the crane's tower taller, right?" Fuerth asked Samuels. (On high-rise construction jobs, the crane's tower sometimes needs to be heightened so it can reach higher floors.)

Samuels replied that the crane crew used a different method to accomplish this task, one that did *not* require the safeties to be deactivated. "Even if we *had* needed to disable them," he had testified previously, "the crane crew wouldn't have been able to. We would have had to ask New York Crane to do it, either by changing a relay in the crane's electrical cabinet, or by changing the crane's computer program."

"But you could have removed them manually, correct?" asked Fuerth. "You could have taken them off with a wrench, right?"

"Actually, you'd need two wrenches," replied Samuels. But in his thirty years as a crane operator, he added, he had never known anyone to remove these switches manually.

I wrote in my notebook, "If Samuels has never removed these switches by hand, how come he knows precisely how to do it? Also, were the switches still on the crane after the accident, or were they missing?" The latter is a question that needs to be answered for Fuerth's supposition to be proven, but it wasn't posed at this juncture. I assumed that was because Samuels was not in a position to know one way or the other. I hoped it would be asked and answered at some point down the road.

October 20

Fuerth took a different tack regarding one of the safety switches, called the high-boom switch (because it prevents the boom from being raised too high), when Samuels returned to the stand this morning. Even if it *was* functioning, Fuerth claimed, it had been set incorrectly.

"You and Mr. Leo sometimes raised the boom four degrees higher than the seventy-eight-degree limit mandated by the City's Department of Buildings, right?" Fuerth asked.

"Yes, but we hardly ever needed to," Samuels replied, squirming. "Anyway, eighty-two degrees is the limit permitted in the crane's manual." Samuels added, "I'm actually not sure which angle the safety switch was set at, seventy-eight or something higher."

My seatmate, Guy, shook his head and scribbled in his notebook. Was he thinking what I was thinking, that Samuels knew the switch was improperly set at a higher angle, and that he was claiming ignorance to protect Don, himself, and his employer (Sorbara, the concrete subcontractor)?

Right before Samuels was dismissed by Judge Mendez, Panzella stood up and declared, "Your Honor, I have one more thing I'd like to ask this witness."

For once, the judge hit the brakes on her: "That's it, Ms. Panzella. We're done."

The personalized tote bag she brought to court today may have been inscribed with the words "Legal Diva," but Panzella didn't get special treatment this time.

October 22

Wednesdays, our day off from jury duty, have become a homemaking marathon for me. Today I cleaned, did umpteen loads of laundry, and made a giant lasagna that should keep my family alive for the next few days. I suppose this is how *real* working mothers spend their free time, I thought as I unloaded the dishwasher.

In the name of jury duty, as alluded to previously, I've set aside my hobbies. I've had coffee just once with a mom friend who works part-time. And my internet activity has been curtailed dramatically (probably a good thing).

But the one extracurricular I've refused to give up is my daily trip to the gym. Today, I squeezed it in in the early evening, which I do even on jury-duty days. This means that dinner, which I've continued to insist be eaten as a family, has been delayed until at least eight o'clock in the Pigott household. Bob and Jules have started grumbling. "Have an apple!" has become my go-to reply to their cries for mercy.

October 23

To prove that Don Leo was not at fault for the collapse, today Panzella put on another witness: Mark Jansen, a so-called "signalman" whose job, on the Ninety-First Street site, was to tell the crane operators where to pick up and deposit loads.

Just before eight o'clock in the morning on the day of the accident, Jansen testified, he asked Don to position the crane's boom above a crate of electrical supplies. "Don lowered the hoist line down to about thirty or forty feet above this container, and then I told him to wait," Jansen told us. "Right before the accident, the line did not move from this position."

Jansen's testimony directly contradicted one of Fuerth's claims: that Don raised the hoist line too high (so high, in fact, that the headache ball—the device at the end of the line that acts as ballast—collided with the wheel through which the line is wound, thereby destabilizing the crane, and causing it to collapse).

Of course, I realized, Jansen, like Samuels before him, was hardly a disinterested witness. He might have been covering for his dead colleague. "On the other hand," I wrote in my notebook, "Jansen could be biased *and* telling the truth."

October 24

"Panzella was a hairdresser before she became a lawyer!" I overheard one of the jurors tell a seatmate when I arrived this morning.

"That explains why she's so nicely coiffed," our colleague replied.

"Guess how old she is," the informant continued.

"Late fifties?"

"She's sixty-seven!"

"She looks great for her age."

I wondered how our comrade had obtained this information. Through an internet search, I suppose. Wouldn't that be breaking the rule to not research the case (which is why I'm keeping this juror's identity secret)?

Maybe not. After all, Panzella's particulars, I reasoned, including her unconventional path to the law, aren't part of the case per se.

* * *

Having established that Don Leo did *not* cause the accident, Panzella's next move was to prove who *did*. She started with the first defendant named in this lawsuit, Mr. James F. Lomma, the crane's owner.

Her attack began with a witness named Byron Biggerstaff (a name right out of a Charles Dickens novel, I thought). An employee of the City's Department of Investigation, Biggerstaff testified that, on the very same day as the collapse, he went to Lomma's New Jersey headquarters to deliver a search warrant for evidence. When he arrived in the middle of the night, Biggerstaff told us, he was surprised to find a man named Michael Carbone waiting outside.

"Who is Mr. Carbone?" asked Panzella.

"At that time, he was chief inspector for the Cranes and Derricks division of the City's Department of Buildings," Biggerstaff replied.

"Before that, what was Mr. Carbone's job?" Panzella continued.

"He worked for Lomma," Biggerstaff replied.

"Did you ask him what he was doing outside Lomma's office?"

"Yes."

"What did Mr. Carbone say?"

"He told me he was getting a ride to his car."

"And who gave him this ride?"

"A Lomma employee."

"What did you say to Mr. Carbone?" Panzella continued, a sly smile creeping up her face.

"I informed him that it was inappropriate for a crane inspector to get a ride from an employee of a company whose crane had just collapsed," Biggerstaff boomed.

Every head in the jury box shook in response to Carbone's suspiciously improper behavior.

The next witness, Jeremy Rosenberg, an investigator for the Manhattan District Attorney's office, further strengthened Panzella's hand.

"Mr. Rosenberg, did you arrive at New York Crane

headquarters shortly after Mr. Biggerstaff did?" Panzella asked.

"Yes," Rosenberg replied.

"What happened when you got there?" asked Panzella, her grin reaching ever higher.

"I overheard Carbone tell someone, 'You gotta get me outta here!' " Rosenberg answered.

We jurors released a collective gasp. Sounded like something out of a mafia movie, I thought.

Rosenberg and Biggerstaff suspected that Carbone had been summoned by Lomma, his former employer, to destroy any documents that he, as a Department of Buildings insider, would know were incriminating.

Soon after Rosenberg gained access to the building, Lomma himself showed up.

"What did Mr. Lomma tell you?" asked Panzella.

"He said, 'You don't need to rummage through my files. I've already prepared a stack of relevant papers to give you'," Rosenberg replied.

"What did you think about that?"

"It struck me as peculiar. How did Mr. Lomma *know* I was coming to deliver a search warrant?"

To me, it sure sounded like Carbone and Lomma had been in cahoots.

October 28

Over the weekend, I confess, I googled Karten, one of the attorneys for plaintiff Ramadan Kurtaj.

As it turns out, she and Panzella actually have a lot in common. Karten's sixty-six, so they're about the same age. And like Panzella, Karten didn't start out as a lawyer. She was an assistant to a personal injury attorney, then went to law school at night. In fact, she and Panzella both attended Brooklyn Law School (in different classes), graduating in the early nineteen eighties.

Karten's resume includes some newsworthy accomplishments. Karten represented one of the first doctors to get AIDS while treating a patient. She also did a stint on Court TV, commenting on the O.J. Simpson trial.

Karten has some impressive experience under her high-waisted belt.

* * *

Today we heard from our first female witness, a thirtyish woman named Bethany Klein, whose wavy hair was pulled back in an impromptu bun, and who wore a bold brooch on her cowl-neck sweater. After she took the stand, Klein, a former director of the Cranes and Derricks division of the City's Department of Buildings, shot cocksure glances at everyone in the courtroom. This lady's going to be tough-as-nails on Panzella's target, Mr. Lomma, I thought.

Klein testified that the crane at issue in this case had a history of mechanical problems, including a cracked bearing that had been discovered on the job right before the one at Ninety-First Street. (This broken bearing would end up being replaced with the allegedly defective one that the plaintiffs claim killed Don and Ramadan.)

Klein halted work on the site, then required Lomma to hire an engineer to find out what had caused the defect. "Unfortunately, Lomma removed the section of the bearing that contained the crack before this guy could inspect it," said Klein, angered that Lomma had destroyed evidence. Juror Number Four, Erin, a pretty, twenty-something blonde who's a structural engineer in the real world, stifled a gasp. Klein had no choice but to let the engineer do the best he could without the evidentiary crack, and he concluded, based on other indications, that its cause was "consistent with" a lightning strike.

"I questioned that assessment," testified Klein, who later found out that this engineer had a conflict of interest, because he had worked for Lomma in the past. "It seemed likelier that the crack was due to wear-and-tear, since the crane was twenty-three years old." When Panzella intimated that Lomma preferred the lightning-strike scenario because an act of God, unlike wear-and-tear, would be covered by insurance, Mary (Alternate Number One) let out an audible "tsk-tsk."

Klein also instructed Lomma that he had to notify her ahead of time before the bearing was either repaired, or, if it couldn't be fixed (as turned out to be the case), replaced. "I needed to approve the procedure and make sure it was done right," Klein testified.

By the time she left her position at Cranes and Derricks, Klein had not received any such notice, and Lomma never informed her successor about the replacement bearing, either.

* * *

There were now five dark shadows trailing Mr. Lomma, I concluded on my way home. One, his suspicious behavior on the night of the accident. Two, his crane's history of mechanical problems. Three, his willful destruction of evidence (the crack in the original bearing). Four, his possible commitment of insurance fraud. And five, his refusal to play by Cranes and Derricks' rules.

October 29

On our day off, I took our family dog, Scout, to the vet for her annual checkup.

"How are *you* doing?" he asked me while he peered inside Scout's ears.

"Great! I've been on jury duty since the beginning of the month. It's a wrongful-death case, and it's really interesting," I replied.

After posing several questions about the trial that I was permitted to half-answer only, the good doctor shook his head. "Sounds fascinating. But I'd *never* have the time to be a juror."

My extended family, friends, and neighbors have all reacted the same way, and it's started to bother me. Their not-so-subtle message: Before you took on this task, you must have had *way* too much time on your hands. Their critique stung, I realized, because they were right. Once this trial ends, I told myself, I've *got* to get a real job.

October 30

"If Fuerth starts another sentence with 'In terms of,' I think I'm gonna scream," muttered Sandra, Juror Number One (a twenty-something Hispanic woman with dyed red hair who favors bohemian, brightly-colored clothes) while we waited in our hallway this morning.

"I've noticed that, too," I groaned. "It's really aggravating."

"And did you see that dress Karten had on the other day, the one with the metal-ringed holes along the hem?" Sandra continued. "It was so weird."

"It looked like an upside-down shower curtain," I joked. (A cruel quip, I admit: But when you observe the same group of people for six hours, day after day, even their minor eccentricities become fodder for mockery. What's more, I wouldn't be surprised if the attorneys made fun of us jurors, too—and I wouldn't blame them, either.)

Once we'd all arrived, Melanie led our merry band toward the courtroom, but stopped short, opening a side door instead. Wonder of wonder, miracle of miracles: God (Judge Mendez, that is) has given us our very own jury room!

It was nothing special. An aging poster of a generic landscape hung on its cracked, off-white walls, and it was filled with an old wooden (of course) table surrounded by a baker's dozen of rickety chairs. There was also a small, elevated window through which, like prisoners, we could spy a patch of sky. Humble though they were, our new digs gave us some welcome privacy, unlike the hallway, where we'd felt like our every move was watched, and our every utterance was overheard.

Once we'd settled in, one of the jurors, apparently comfortable breaking the "no discussing the case" rule now that we had a hideaway, said, "Lomma's a bad guy."

I buried my head in my newspaper, pretending not to have heard.

Another juror replied, "You're right. He's a money-grubbing crook."

I looked up to find other members of our group nodding.

It seemed that several jurors had already succumbed to Lomma's bad-guy image, the one that Panzella, in particular, has repeatedly drummed into our heads.

* * *

Today's witness brought us to the crux of the plaintiffs' case against Lomma: his procurement of the replacement crane bearing with the allegedly faulty weld.

One of Lomma's mechanics, a Hungarian immigrant named Tibor Varganyi (pronounced TEE-bore Var-GONE-yee), began his testimony in broken English and with a thick accent. For someone in his seventies, I thought, he has a remarkably full head of hair, with a precisely trimmed mustache to boot. He resembles the Wizard of Oz, I realized.

Varganyi's principal job, he explained, was to service Lomma's tower cranes, in particular the model at issue in this case, called a Kodiak. Lomma had bought several cranes of this type secondhand, including the one that collapsed at Ninety-First Street, and Varganyi knew their ins and outs because he had worked for the cranes' previous owner as well.

"Let's talk about your involvement in the criminal case," Panzella told Varganyi threateningly. That's right, I'd almost forgotten: Judge Mendez told us that there had been a criminal trial against Lomma and his businesses (but *not* the other defendants in this trial) two years ago, in 2012, regarding this same accident.

"On October 5, 2011, did you enter a pre–criminal-trial plea?" asked Panzella.

"Yes," replied Varganyi, nervously rubbing together the thumb and forefinger of his right hand.

"Did you plead guilty to criminally negligent homicide?"

"Yes."

"Why?"

"Because I'm the one who ordered the bearing with the bad weld that caused the accident."

I gasped at this straight-out confession, as did my seatmates.

"Did you go to prison?"

"No."

"What was your punishment?"

"I did a year of community service."

"Why such a light sentence?"

"I agreed to testify against Mr. Lomma."

"Was your boss found guilty?"

"No. The judge found Lomma not guilty." (It had been a so-called "bench trial," in which the judge renders the verdict.)

Panzella shook her head in disgust at what she deemed a clear miscarriage of justice. The jurors narrowed their eyes in puzzlement. If Varganyi pled guilty, then it goes without saying that the bearing, not operator error, caused the accident (unless Varganyi pled guilty to something he didn't do because he was too scared to go to trial). And if Varganyi was guilty, shouldn't his boss, on whose behalf he bought the defective part, have been found guilty in that trial—and automatically be found liable in this one?

* * *

Tonight, I researched O'Neill, one of the attorneys for the Kurtaj estate. As I'd suspected, he's from the Midwest, a native Michigander like I am. He majored in Classics at the University of Michigan, where he graduated fourth in his class. I'd never imagined a personal injury attorney to be a brainiac who spent his undergraduate years with the likes of Homer and Cicero.

O'Neill got his law degree at Wayne State University in Detroit, moved to New York, and eventually started his own firm, specializing in employment discrimination (which explains why he doesn't fit either of my personal-injury stereotypes). How did he end up on the Kurtaj case, I wondered?

October 31

A fat pumpkin, care of Martha, greeted me when I entered our newly-bestowed jury room this morning.

To celebrate Halloween, the table was also festooned with two huge bowls of candy, a treat from Judge Mendez. I gobbled up a piece or two, then snuck a few more into the courtroom, where I unwrapped each one, hidden under my notebook, as quietly as possible, then popped it in my mouth under the guise of stifling a yawn. (Mendez forbids food and drinks, except water, in the courtroom. One of the jurors joked that he's going to spike his water bottle with vodka.)

My seatmate, Guy, whispered, "Since it's Halloween, maybe the lawyers will entertain us with a spine-tingling story today."

Guy's remark, though sarcastic, got me thinking about the story-telling aspect of this trial. Each attorney's carefully crafted tale likely *ex*cludes inconvenient truths, and *in*cludes only convenient truths. If we jurors pick and choose the truths that seem most convincing, when put together will they reveal the *whole* truth? Maybe not. That's likely what many of the trial's "sidebars" (when the judge asks the lawyers to approach for a private discussion) are about: what we jurors can and cannot be told.

It was an irksome realization. Can our verdict, indeed *any* verdict, be legitimate if it's not based on the whole truth? (The very word "verdict" comes from the Anglo-French word *veirdit*, *veir* meaning true, and *dit* meaning statement.) I guess I'll have to trust that the law, developed over the centuries, will steer us right.

* * *

When Varganyi, Lomma's mechanic, retook the stand, he attempted to justify a questionable, allegedly deadly, decision on his part: ordering a new bearing for the crane at the heart of this case from an unknown manufacturer in China instead of a reputable company in the U.S.

After the American manufacturer of the machine's original bearing told him it would take two years to provide a replacement—a wait that would have cost his boss more than one million dollars in lost crane rental revenue—Varganyi decided to see if he could get one quick. He did a Google search, as if he were shopping for a sweater, and came across a Chinese bearing company called RTR. (The acronym, nonsensically, stands for "Road to Rome.")

"It was a nice-looking website," Varganyi told Panzella matter-of-factly, as if its polished appearance excused all the trouble that followed. He reached out to a woman named Joyce Wang, RTR's contact person, to inquire about purchasing a crane bearing. So began a lengthy email exchange that revealed a frightening ignorance of basic engineering principles—as well as the English language—on the part of both Varganyi and Wang.

Eventually, Wang gave Varganyi the good news: Not only would she deliver a new bearing in a mere three months, but she would also charge the bargain-basement price of twenty thousand dollars. (An American-made bearing would have cost at least five times that amount.) "Please send me a pro forma invoice and I start the money rolling!" replied an overjoyed Varganyi.

Later, however, Wang issued a warning. "Hi Tibor," she wrote. "Just discuss with our general manager. He said the last time we did only the bearing and didn't weld and the customer weld itself. He said because in the crane it is a very important part and we are afraid the weld technique we had is not good because normally we didn't do like that. *And honest speaking, we don't have confidence on this welding* [my italics]. So he suggest if you can weld the band yourself."

Panzella, hands trembling, barely contained her righteous ire as Varganyi read aloud this incriminating statement.

November 7

"I've always wanted to learn how to fire a gun," I heard Alternate Number Two, whose name is Kayla, tell cops Tony and Aaron while we waited for the trial to resume this morning.

"Next time I go to the NYPD's practice range, I'll sneak you in with me," Tony replied mischievously.

"You've got guts," I told Kayla.

Picking up on the note of admiration in my voice, this thirty-something juror, clad in a black leather jacket, black jeans, and skull earrings, started a conversation with me. "What do you do for a living?" Kayla asked.

"I'm a stay-at-home mom," I replied, feeling like even more of a wuss.

"I have two jobs," replied Kayla, whose perfectly symmetrical face was framed by a black ponytail swept dramatically to one side. "I'm a freelance fitness and nutrition consultant." That explains the ridiculously healthy-looking, gray-green concoction Kayla downs every morning in the jury room. "I'm also a deejay on a hard-rock radio program."

Could this woman be any cooler? I thought.

* * *

Varganyi, the crane owner's mechanic, retook the stand, and we found out that, despite Wang's heads-up, Varganyi asked RTR to do the weld anyway, for which Lomma paid almost two thousand dollars extra. What's more, Varganyi ordered two additional bearings from RTR, to replace other bearings in his boss's Kodiak cranes.

When the first Chinese bearing was delivered to New York Crane in December 2007, Varganyi testified, he unwrapped it, then looked for the much-discussed weld. Because the Chinese company had machined it to make it look "smooth and pretty," as Varganyi described it, it was no longer visible to the naked eye.

"The bearing looked like it was made of just one piece of steel," Varganyi said.

"What did Mr. Lomma say?" asked Panzella.

"I didn't tell him," replied Varganyi sheepishly.

"If Lomma had come to you and said, 'I paid extra for a weld. Where is it?', what would have happened?"

"He would have been mad."

Instead, Varganyi told Panzella, he went ahead and sent the bearing to Brady Marine, the company that would do additional welding to attach the bearing to the bottom of the crane's turntable.

The second RTR bearing (intended for a different crane to be used on another construction site), Varganyi told Karten in her examination, arrived in April 2008. This time the Chinese weld was clearly visible.

"What did you think when you saw it?" asked Karten.

"It was a piss poor job. Excuse my language," replied Varganyi.

Once again, Varganyi said nothing about it to his higher-ups at New York Crane, and once again he sent the bearing directly to Brady Marine. The Brady workers recognized immediately that the weld was bad, and contacted Lomma to alert him to the problem.

"Had the first RTR bearing already been installed in the Kodiak crane?" Karten asked.

"Yes," replied Varganyi.

"Had that crane already been erected on Ninety-First Street?"

"Yes."

"Was it in operation yet?"

"No."

"Did Lomma tell you to go to Ninety-First Street and say, 'Wait, don't start using this crane until we double-check its bearing?' "

"No."

"Did you, Mr. Varganyi, feel any moral responsibility to go over there of your own volition? To tell the workers, 'Take that crane down. Let's look at it. Let's make sure.' "

"Objection, Judge, that's not a question," interjected Fuerth, his bald pate turning crimson.

"Sustained," replied Mendez.

"What about you, sir?" Karten continued.

"No," replied Varganyi. "It wasn't my company. It wasn't my decision. Sorry. I'm just a two-hundred-and-fifty-pound Homo sapiens. I'm not a god, okay?"

When Panzella (in re-cross) asked Varganyi, for the millionth time, if *anyone* at New York Crane had considered the second RTR bearing, with the obviously defective weld, to be a red flag to recheck the first one, he threw up his hands.

"Ms. Panzella, there is one more thing that I *must* tell you. That before the crane went out it had been inspected by New York City—".

"Objection, your Honor," growled Karten.

"Sustained," replied Mendez, scowling at the witness for flouting that cardinal rule of courtroom discourse: Just answer the question, no less, no more.

Varganyi's effort to justify his company's inaction—that the City's Department of Buildings had inspected and approved the crane—was stricken from the record.

The Kodiak crane began working at Ninety-First Street on April 24, 2008. On May 30, it collapsed. On June 4, Varganyi sent his last email to Wang: "Stop production of the third bearing and return our deposit." He didn't even tell her why.

* * *

Things are looking really bad for the New York Crane folks, I thought on my way home. When Lomma takes the stand, he'll need to conjure his better angel (assuming he has one) to dig himself out of the hole in which Varganyi, whose kooky image doesn't help matters, has buried him.

But then I wondered why the City was getting off scot-free. Didn't its Cranes and Derricks department bear *some* responsibility for missing the alleged mechanical problem when it inspected the crane? And if operator error was to blame, this department should still be on the hook: Another Cranes and Derricks employee, who took the stand after Klein did, had admitted that one of their inspectors had allowed this crane's high-boom safety switch to be set at eighty-two degrees, four degrees higher than the seventy-eight-degree limit set by his own department.

Come to think of it, what about RTR, the Chinese company that manufactured the possibly defective bearing? It committed the (alleged) original sin here. Why wasn't RTR a defendant?

December 1

During our Thanksgiving break, I researched Fuerth, Lomma's lead lawyer. Sure enough, he's the straight shooter he appears to be. After graduating from Fordham Law School in New York City in the late nineteen seventies, Fuerth has spent his entire career at the same law firm, making partner and specializing in litigation of the type in which he's now embroiled. I wrote "embroiled" because he wasn't having an easy time of it, despite his fine education and steady career.

* * *

Varganyi retook the stand, to be cross-examined by Fuerth. Since Panzella had made this witness look like an ignorant buffoon, Fuerth's first order of business was to convince the jury that this eccentric mechanic with an eighth-grade education really *did* have the necessary know-how to order a crucial crane component.

"Tibor, you used the process of reverse engineering to order the bearing, correct?" Fuerth asked.

"Yes," he replied.

"Can you please explain that process to the jury?" Fuerth continued, licking his lips in anticipation of a cogent reply.

"Now that you mention it, when they killed Osama Bin Laden, a helicopter went down, and they were afraid the bad guys would take the chopper and reverse engineer it," was Varganyi's out-of-left-field answer.

All the jurors sat up. Huh? Why was Varganyi talking about an infamous terrorist in the middle of a trial about a crane accident?

Stepping in to clarify, Fuerth asked, "That would be an *example* of reverse engineering, right?"

Beaming proudly, Varganyi replied, "An example, yeah. You like it?"

"I gotta love ya, Tibor!" Fuerth exclaimed.

I stole a glance at Don Leo's mother, who was scowling. Obviously, *she* didn't love the man whom she believed killed her son.

"Objection, your Honor," boomed Panzella, slamming one of her pastel-colored folders down on the table in front of her. I guess she thought Fuerth was trying to exploit Varganyi's quirkiness to make him look harmless.

Panzella shouldn't have worried: If this was Fuerth's plan B (plan A, making him look competent, having failed), it wasn't working on me. I was still haunted by my initial, mean-old-man impression of Varganyi: Toward the beginning of his testimony, Varganyi said he once told two workers (neither was Don Leo), whom he felt were mishandling his boss's crane, to "jump to their deaths."

In any case, Fuerth then turned to plan C: He suggested that, because of personal experience, Varganyi was intimately concerned about crane safety.

"You yourself were once in a terrible construction accident, right?" Fuerth asked.

"Yes," Varganyi replied.

"What happened?"

"I was in a crane when it suddenly tipped over because the turntable bolts snapped. I almost died. I couldn't work for years."

I wrote in my notebook, "If Varganyi is so concerned

about safety, if he thinks he did such a good job, if he's so innocent, then why did he plead guilty in the criminal trial?" Varganyi's plea, plus his incriminating testimony in this trial, amounted to a high hurdle for Fuerth, his boss's attorney, to surmount.

When I looked up, I saw that Alison, Alternate Number Six, was also scribbling furiously. She wasn't, however, taking notes. A thirtyish, fine-featured artist with blond hair and piercing blue eyes, Alison has taken to drawing in her notebook, filling its pages with portraits of the proceeding's participants (some of which are reproduced in this book). She's shown them to us jurors to lift our spirits as the going has gotten tougher—and longer.

* * *

The jury has started to worry that the trial will take more than three months. For one thing, most of the sixteen attorneys feel compelled to get in their two cents during direct, redirect, cross-, and re-cross examinations, even if they don't have anything new to add. (I guess they figure they better do *something* to justify their high-priced services to their clients.) This means each witness is on the stand for hours, if not days.

"The lawyers waste so much time, repeating one another's arguments," complained Erin back in the jury room.

"Plus Mendez lets them go on and on forever," chimed in Shawn (Alternate Number Five), a fortyish Black man whose broad smile and pinchable cheeks bring to mind the longtime *Saturday Night Live* cast member Kenan Thompson.

"And having Wednesdays off is a mixed blessing," added Martha. "It's nice to have time off, but it makes the case drag on longer."

"This is gonna be a four-season trial," predicted Tony. "We won't be done until summer next year."

Aisha balled up a piece of paper and threw it at him. "Don't even *think* that," she teased him.

If it's going to be longer than three months, I can handle it, I thought. I'm fortunate that my life "on the outside" has not been unduly hampered. I'm finding the trial's subject matter really interesting. I'm learning a lot about the law (and, for that matter, human nature). Plus, I have a confession to make: It's a power trip to sit in judgment, particularly for yours truly, a stay-at-home mom who hasn't wielded much clout over the last two decades.

What's more, my fellow jurors are good company. No irritating scolds, no pushy know-it-alls. And despite our different backgrounds, we're getting along well. Everyone is funny (or enjoys a joke); everyone is respectful (of one another, if not of the lawyers or witnesses); and everyone is easy-going (so far).

No bad apples. Let's hope deliberations—if I get to take part in them—won't reveal any rotten spots.

December 2

"Somehow, we ended up in a lesbian bar," I overheard Alison tell Tony when I entered the jury room this morning.

Alison and Sandra, who both work in the fashion

industry and are close in age, have bonded to such a degree that they now socialize outside the courthouse. Last Saturday, the two of them went club-hopping, and ended up in a hangout where, being heterosexual, they felt out of place.

"How could you tell it was a lesbian bar—other than the fact that there were no men around?" asked Tony.

"Trust me," Alison replied, "I went to a women's college, so I know a lesbian when I see one."

"Which college?" I interrupted.

"Smith."

"I went there, too!"

Several "Smithies" (as graduates of this college, one of the renowned Seven Sisters, are called) live in New York City. But since it's a small school, the chances of two ending up on the same jury are slim. While Alison and I explored our coincidental connection, Aisha, the only juror who not only didn't go to college, but didn't finish high school, looked up from her phone, shrugged, and didn't even try to understand what all the fuss was about.

It turned out that college wasn't the only thing Alison and I had in common.

"My 'mum' is British, so I travelled to England a lot as a child," Alison told me.

"I have a British connection, too!" I replied. "My parents and I lived in England in the nineteen seventies!"

I think I may have found my BJFF (Best Juror Friend Forever).

* * *

On my way home, my courthouse and real-world lives collided. It was particularly cold out, so I took the bus from my subway stop instead of walking the seven long blocks to my apartment building. After I sat down, I recognized a witness from the trial. (I didn't write about this particular one in my diary because I'd found his testimony unbelievable.) He took a seat right in front of mine as I slunk behind my newspaper.

He was with his mother (I knew who she was because she had attended the trial during her son's testimony), and he didn't seem to have noticed me. I admit that I broke the rules big-time and eavesdropped on their conversation, hoping this witness might say something more forthright than he had when he was on the stand. Unfortunately, they spoke in Spanish (which I studied for a year, but I'm rusty); no matter, since, as far as I could make out, all they discussed was dinner plans.

* * *

During *our* dinner, I told Bob and Jules about my close encounter. Jules excused herself before I'd even finished my tale. I was miffed: I know she's got homework, I thought, but can't she express a modicum of interest in a story related to my newfound "purpose"?

At least my husband was listening. When I'd finished my tale, I worried, "Did I just break the rule against discussing the case?"

"No," he assured me. "All you did was describe how

61

you bumped into a witness. It's not like you told me what he said in court and asked my opinion."

Bob was right. So I let loose and served him more trial-related tidbits: How one of the lawyers (Fuerth) has a bald patch that reddens when he's annoyed with a particular opponent (Panzella); how another attorney never sits up straight (O'Neill); and how one of the jurors (Tony) stands up in the jury box from time to time. (The first time Tony did this, I thought he was going to walk out on the trial. As it turned out, Tony has a bad back, and Judge Mendez gave him permission to stretch periodically.)

I think Bob enjoyed hearing about my new world. Since abandoning my magazine career to become a full-time mom, my topics of conversation have been limited: the latest crises at our kids' schools; the latest painting I've finished; the latest book I'm reading; or the latest *New York Times* headline that grabbed my attention. Jury duty has, thankfully, provided me with an interesting experience to talk about.

I realized, however, that it was going to be really hard to resist crossing the line, to not enter into a true "discussion of the case." Luckily, Bob's a lawyer, so he knows precisely where to draw that line. I can count on him to keep me in the safe zone.

December 4

The big kahuna, the man Panzella derisively calls "the King of Cranes," finally took the stand this morning.

As the seventyish James F. Lomma lumbered down the aisle, leaning on a cane, everyone stared, like rubber-neckers on a highway. Unfortunately for Lomma (and his struggling attorneys), his impaired gait did not make him more sympathetic, but rather more akin to the consummate Bond villain.

Defendant James F. Lomma. *Courtroom Sketch by Juror Alison Colby.*

Lomma's considerable height made him appear not statuesque, but looming. Shoe-polish dyed black hair eclipsed his doughy face, and his mouth was set in a permanent sneer above his double chin. Atop his long nose rested a pair of ominous-looking tinted glasses. During a break, Shawn commented, "He looks like Jim Jones, the cult leader who convinced his followers to drink poison-laced Kool-Aid."

This first impression, I thought, is going to make it extremely hard for me *not* to jump on the jury's anti-Lomma bandwagon.

* * *

Panzella paced back and forth as she fired questions at Lomma.

"Let's see if we can start off by agreeing on a few things," said Panzella. "Do you agree that tower cranes are not supposed to fall from the sky?"

"I agree," Lomma replied robotically.

"Do you believe that every work site, no matter where it is, in the City of New York, across the country, across the world, must be safely equipped, no excuses, no exceptions?"

"I agree."

Panzella's opening line of questioning continued in this vein, and it came across as posturing to me. Just get on with it, I wished I could tell her.

As she examined Lomma, Panzella got closer and closer, like a lioness stalking her prey, until she was actually resting her arm on the witness stand.

"Objection, judge, she's crowding the witness," Fuerth complained.

"Sorry, your Honor," Panzella apologized. She retreated to look for a document in her now overflowing stacks of folders.

"Find that email," Panzella ordered one of the attorneys at her side.

"Sure, Mom," he replied.

"Mom?!" Did I hear that right? During a break, I asked my fellow jurors if they had heard it, too.

"The lawyer we've been calling Antonio [because he looks like the actor Antonio Banderas] is Panzella's *son?!*" exclaimed Sandra.

"I can't believe he called her 'Mom' in front of us," added another juror. "That's so unprofessional."

"I also can't believe he lets her boss him around like that," I said.

* * *

Back in the courtroom, Panzella showed Lomma a video of Don Leo operating the crane at the site where the accident later occurred.

"How much does that bucket of concrete in the film weigh?" Panzella asked Lomma.

"It's not my job to know what it weighs," Lomma replied in a voice as monotone as Fuerth's.

"Where are they pouring that concrete?"

"I dunno."

"Have you ever even *been* on a concrete superstructure building site?"

"No."

So what? I thought. He supplies cranes, not concrete. Why should he know this stuff?

"Mr. Lomma, are you taking any medications—or is

there anything else—that would prevent you from answering my questions?" Panzella asked with a smirk.

"No," he replied.

I was surprised that Fuerth didn't object to this personal query, and wondered what Panzella was getting at. Surely her intention couldn't have been to help him, to provide him with an excuse for his ignorance. Maybe she was emphasizing his incompetence. Or perhaps she was being sarcastic: "Mr. Lomma, if you can't answer my questions, you must be high."

December 9

After three and a half days of repeating ad nauseam her accusations of negligence, Panzella finally finished examining Lomma today.

A premier example of her time wasting: "Here are four hundred and fifty pages of New York Crane's maintenance records for the crane that collapsed," Panzella declared, dumping the tome on the witness stand. "Sir, I want you to look through it and find an inspection report for the replacement bearing."

Lomma turned each page nonchalantly, and after about fifteen minutes, he asked, "Should I keep going?"

"Yes," commanded Panzella.

He shrugged, and continued for another half hour, coming up empty-handed. While Lomma searched in vain, Guy and I resorted to playing Hangman in our notebooks.

Other than the hard-earned revelation that New York

Crane had never inspected the crane's replacement bearing, Panzella still didn't prove that Lomma *knew* that Varganyi had ordered it in an incompetent manner. Panzella also didn't prove that Lomma failed to notify Cranes and Derricks about the new bearing because he was afraid the department would give it a thumbs-down.

Panzella did, however, produce an incriminating document from the criminal case against Lomma. In 2010, one of Lomma's lawyers had told the Manhattan District Attorney, "RTR manufactured a bearing with a defective weld," in an attempt to have the charges against his client dropped by putting one hundred percent of the blame on the Chinese manufacturer.

Hold on, I thought: If Lomma's attorney knew the weld was bad, Lomma himself must have known as well. But that was 2010, two years *after* the accident. It still didn't prove that Lomma knew about it *before* the accident.

Then I thought: Maybe that doesn't matter. If Lomma didn't know, I reasoned, he *should* have. If you're going to trust a numskull like Varganyi to order an essential crane component, you'd better keep a close eye on him.

December 11

"As you sit here today, and after having answered my questions, do you feel you have *any* responsibility for the deaths of Ramadan Kurtaj and Donald Leo?' Karten, one of the Kurtaj attorneys, asked Lomma at the end of her direct examination.

"I dunno," Lomma replied, pushing his freshly-blackened hair off his forehead.

The jurors raised their eyebrows at Lomma's weak-kneed response. Did he just admit that he might be at fault? His reply finally scored a point for Karten, whose follow-up to Panzella hadn't covered much new territory. (To be fair, the latter is hard to accomplish, since Panzella leaves no stone unturned in her examinations.) Unfortunately, when Karten asked Lomma if he would have gone forward with the RTR welding if he *had* seen Wang's "no confidence" email (to which he also replied "I dunno"), she lost a point by conceding that he had *not* seen this correspondence before the accident.

* * *

While we were packing up in the jury room, a tall, slender woman with rimless glasses and short, layered hair marched in with an air of authority. "Hi, I'm Irene, the supervising jury clerk in Room 452," she announced with a smug smile. "I'm here to answer your questions about your paychecks."

Those of us who aren't paid regular salaries by an employer during jury duty get a whopping forty dollars a day from the State of New York. At first our checks had arrived every two weeks like clockwork, but recently they've been late, plus we've occasionally been underpaid. Some of the jurors have complained, which, I assume, led to this honcho's visit.

"Our payment system has been undergoing some changes," Irene explained. "Everything should be fixed soon."

Satisfied that we'd been mollified without letting anyone ask a single question, Irene turned sharply on her stiletto heels and was about to leave when Alison, piqued that this woman had given us short shrift, laid into her.

"We were told the trial would last three months but there's no end in sight and why were we lied to and how am I supposed to do my job and serve on a jury and when is it going to end?"

"Your employer is paying you, so I don't know why you're complaining," Irene replied curtly.

Alison retorted, "It's not just about the money it's about doing my job well and impressing my bosses and not stalling the momentum of my career because of some trial that has nothing to do with me."

Irene was having none of it. She made a quick exit, leaving us to console Alison. I didn't blame her for being angry: If I were her, I'd have quit the trial long ago, or never volunteered in the first place.

December 12

We lost our first juror today. But it wasn't Alison.

During a break, Mary, Alternate Number One, went to the bathroom, and she never returned. Melanie escorted the rest of us back into the courtroom with no explanation, and we continued without Mary. What happened? we wondered. Was she taken ill?

Melanie later explained, "Mary left her purse in the ladies' room by mistake, and when she went back to get it, it was gone." Understandably upset, Mary didn't want to return to the courtroom unless it was found, and Judge Mendez had decided to dismiss her from the jury.

I wasn't sorry to see her leave. Mary seemed perfectly nice, but she'd kept to herself so much that that she never felt like one of the gang. (All I ever learned about her was that she was a retired school crossing guard.) Besides, now that I'd been "promoted" to Alternate Number Three, I was one step closer to the opportunity to deliberate.

* * *

Back in the courtroom, Fuerth began his cross-examination of Lomma. After reintroducing us to "the King of Cranes," Fuerth posed a series of questions, about the logistics of Lomma's companies, whose relevance eluded me: which ones own cranes, which ones are involved in trucking operations, which ones pay which employees, and so on.

My befuddled boredom exacerbated my physical discomfort. (The jury box chairs were obviously built before ergonomics became a thing). I was overwhelmed by the urge to stand up and ask, "What does any of this have to do with the accident?"

But jurors, like children, are to be seen and not heard, so I swallowed hard, remained seated, and closed my eyes in silent protest.

When Fuerth finally moved on to a different line of questioning, I paid attention.

"Right after you found out about the collapse, how did you feel?" he asked Lomma.

"I was very concerned because people had been hurt or killed," he replied. "Marino and Carmela Sorbara [the concrete company's owners] were very upset, just like I was. We didn't know what had happened. And we just spent a couple of hours consoling one another."

During that conversation, Lomma told the Sorbaras that "they had done nothing wrong," an absolution that the plaintiffs' lawyers—who seem to consider Lomma Public Enemy Number One, and the other defendants lesser antagonists—had pounced on during their direct examinations. But Fuerth claimed that Lomma did not mean to suggest that the Sorbara *company* was blameless.

"What, if anything, did you discuss with Marino about who was at fault for the collapse?" Fuerth asked.

"I just told him that he wasn't personally—it wasn't anything he did personally. It was an accident. It was nothing he did."

"What, if anything, was going through your mind about legal issues and lawsuits?"

"Nothing."

Nonsense, I thought: If Lomma's such a great businessperson, wouldn't "legal issues" have been at the forefront of his mind?

After he got to the accident site, Lomma claimed, he took a look at the debris to try to figure out what had happened. "Most of the crane parts had fallen on the south side of the crane's tower," Lomma told Fuerth. "But I found the headache ball on the north side."

A cavalcade of lawyers stood up to object. Why were they so hot under the collar? I wondered. Mendez allowed each of them to conduct a *voir dire,* which in this context means questioning a witness to determine if he or she is competent to testify about a particular piece of evidence. Panzella suggested that the wreckage could have been moved before Lomma got there, and Karten doubted Lomma's ability to remember a detail such as the location of the headache ball.

"Do you remember this clearly?" Karten asked.

"Clear as a bell," Lomma replied confidently.

"Clear as a bell," Karten repeated with heavy sarcasm.

I guess the headache ball's location somehow suggests operator error, and that's why the plaintiffs' lawyers didn't like Lomma opining on it.

At the end of his examination, Fuerth addressed the elephant in the room: the plea deal Varganyi had taken before the criminal trial began, which would seem to implicate Lomma as well.

"When you learned that Varganyi had taken a plea, what was your reaction?" Fuerth asked.

"I was very upset," Lomma replied.

"What was the reason for that?"

"Because I felt he hadn't done anything wrong."

"What about New York Crane, J.F. Lomma, Inc., or you yourself?"

"We'd done nothin' wrong either."

"Instead of drawing attention to Varganyi's pre-criminal-trial guilty plea, why doesn't Fuerth make more of the fact that his client, Mr. Lomma, was found *not guilty?*" I wrote in my notebook. To my mind, Fuerth was not wielding this weapon as often as he should.

December 15

For Christmas, his Honor gave us a three-week vacation. Most of the jurors don't have big plans for the holidays, and are annoyed that this time off will further postpone the trial's end date.

While we gathered our belongings in the jury room, I realized that this would be the longest break since the trial began. As the case has dragged on, we jurors have adopted a siege mentality that has brought us even closer together. I'll miss my new "family," particularly Alison, my fellow Smithie, and Guy, whom I've dubbed my "jury husband" (like a "work husband").

I'll also miss the simple pleasure of working with others toward a common goal, something I haven't done since my days working at the magazine.

Before I left, I stole a glance at the pumpkin Martha had brought in for Halloween and wondered why no one had thought to replace it with a more seasonal decoration.

January 5, 2015

Let's get this show on the road, I thought as I darted down the hallway on our first morning back. I found Martha—first to arrive as always—sitting at our jury room table with her hands resting on a big box.

"I was spring cleaning during the break," she explained, "and when I came across this jigsaw puzzle, I almost threw it out. But then I thought, why not bring it here? It will give us something to do while we wait around."

"Great idea!" I replied, and we dug right in. It depicted Vincent van Gogh's painting *Café Terrace at Night*. "These cobblestones are gonna be tough," I commented. As the other jurors trickled in, some were intrigued—Erin and Aisha in particular—while others were indifferent. I was of the "separate the edge pieces first" school, others took the "get the easy parts out of the way" approach, and a few plunged in arbitrarily.

Would our different approaches to putting a puzzle together be mirrored in our approaches to putting a verdict together? I wondered.

* * *

Back in the courtroom, Judge Mendez wished us a Happy New Year, then reminded us that we were still in the middle of Lomma's cross-examination. Next up: Alan Kaminsky, an attorney for the construction project's code-veloper and general contractor, DeMatteis. He announced proudly, "My New Year's resolution is to pose only questions that have not already been asked." A promise he would eventually break.

In his examination, Kaminsky took Lomma a step further than Karten had when she asked him if he might have been concerned about the first RTR weld if he had seen the "no confidence in this weld" email from Wang *before* the accident. To Karten, he had responded, "I dunno." To Kaminsky, he replied, "I would have, yes." I glanced at Fuerth for his reaction to his client's misguided confession, but he didn't even look up from his binder.

When Slattery, the counsel for Sorbara (the concrete subcontractor), questioned Lomma about his search for post-accident evidence, it was clear that Lomma was interested *only* in debris that suggested blame on the part of Don Leo, and *not* on his own part.

"On the day of the accident," Slattery asked Lomma, "you decided to walk around the site and look for alternative theories to the failed weld, correct?"

"I dunno," mumbled Lomma.

"Tell me, what *did* you do on that day to investigate the failed weld?"

"When they took the crane down, I took a look at the weld."

"This was *after* you'd already made a determination that the accident was caused by operator error, correct?"

"I had no idea what had caused the accident at that point."

"Didn't you tell the jury that when you got to the scene,

you saw various pieces of evidence that indicated operator error? For example, the location of the headache ball?"

"That was a possibility, correct."

"It was a possibility that you followed up on, right?"

"Yes, I did."

"But you *didn't* follow up on the possibility that the weld failed because it had been improperly manufactured, right?" Slattery continued indignantly.

"I'm not qualified to do that," Lomma stated, stepping into Slattery's trap.

"You *are* qualified to make a determination that the operator caused the accident, but *not* that the weld failed because it had been improperly manufactured?"

"The—all I was able to do was look at the damaged parts," Lomma responded lamely.

Slattery did such a good job the first time around that he passed on re-cross-examination, a gutsy, time-saving move I wished more of the lawyers would make.

January 22

After Lomma's testimony wrapped up, it seemed to me that the plaintiffs' attorneys could move on to their next task: proving liability on the part of the rest of the defendants.

But I'd forgotten that the plaintiffs' lawyers had one final claim to prove in order to nail Lomma: that the Chinese weld was indeed defective. To do so, we were treated to ten days of tedious testimony, finally ending this afternoon, from three "expert" witnesses—scientists with knowledge of structural engineering in general, and welding in particular.

They claimed that the Chinese weld was too small, badly shaped, full of cracks, and incompletely fused.

Why one witness couldn't have proved these claims in half a day or less was beyond me.

* * *

During the testimony of a particularly dull expert, I took a long look at the members of the audience.

On the plaintiffs' side, in the front row, sat Maria Leo, Don's mother. She has attended every single day of the trial, always paying careful attention, always tastefully dressed, and always wearing a large photo pin of her dead son. Today, she was accompanied by an extremely sun-tanned blonde whose identity was unknown to me.

Toward the back sat—or perhaps I should say slouched—Ramadan Kurtaj's widow, whose name is Selvi Sinanovic (pronounced SEL-vee Si-NAN-ow-vik). She shows up only sporadically, which is probably for the best, since she spends most of her time with her eyes either closed or on her cell phone. Luckily for the plaintiffs' case, Mrs. Leo's perfect image outweighs the negative impression Selvi makes.

The defendants' side was empty, as is usually the case. It would help counteract Lomma's bad-guy persona, I thought, if Fuerth asked a few supportive family members or friends to attend from time to time. (The press, who typically sit on either side in the back, are easy to spot because of their reporters' notebooks.)

Then I turned my attention to the lawyers. I noticed that Charles Strugatz, the attorney for the owner of the land where the condominium and school were being built, was missing from the end of the defendants' crowded L-shaped table. I nudged Guy, who reminded me that he's been AWOL for a while, and that the judge had instructed us jurors not to speculate about the reason for his departure. But speculate I must: Did the plaintiffs settle with or dismiss his client?

"Why can't we be told why Strugatz left?" I wrote in my second notebook. (An inveterate note taker, I've already filled my first one.) Oh well. At least things will go more quickly with one fewer lawyer in the room, I thought.

Hope springs eternal.

January 27

At long last it was time for the plaintiffs' lawyers to pin blame on the other defendants: the developers, the general contractor, the concrete subcontractor, and the welder.

They started with the first two groups, with whom they dealt quickly and ineffectively. I was left with the impression that the developers and general contractor were *way* too far removed from the defining moments in this case—the rental of the crane (if its weld caused the accident) and the hiring of its operator (if Don caused it)—to possibly be liable.

* * *

The plaintiffs' attorneys' questioning of these two groups was not, however, a total waste of time: It provided some comic relief, particularly two zingers from Panzella.

When a witness for the general contractor, DeMatteis, delivered an answer she found contemptible, Panzella exclaimed "Humph!" so loudly that everyone could hear her.

"Judge, objection to the 'Humph!' " intoned Mark Levi, a DeMatteis attorney.

"Sustained," replied Mendez. "The jurors will disregard the 'Humph!' "

Everyone in the courtroom laughed unrestrainedly at this interjection, which should find its place in the annals of superlative trial technique.

Panzella inadvertently delivered another moment of levity when she asked this witness to read aloud a list of the rarefied amenities offered by the condominium his company was building.

"Bosch appliances," he began. "Afromosia floors. Concierge services, including dog walking and cat sitting."

"Dog sitting and cat walking," Panzella misrepeated in a derisive tone. I caught Kaminsky's eye, and we both giggled at Panzella's gaffe. Guy nudged me. "Cat walking," he said. "That really *is* exclusive."

Shawn entered the jury room this morning with a wide smile. "I just got the results of my DNA test," he exclaimed. "Now that I know which African countries my ancestors came from, I'd really like to visit them. I'd also like to figure out how my family came to be Catholic."

This comment opened the floodgates to revelations about the jurors' religious leanings. The majority are, or were raised, Catholic; to my astonishment, hard rocker Kayla is a lector at St. Patrick's Cathedral. Guy and I are nonobservant Protestants, while Erin and Alison grew up in secular homes. Not one juror is Jewish (another way they differ from my real-life friends, most of whom are Jewish, as is my husband), Muslim, or of any other faith.

I wondered if our spiritual makeup was influencing our reactions to the witnesses and other players in this trial, or if it would affect our deliberations and verdict? Those of us who are Christians should forgive someone who is truly sorry for his transgressions; but in our capacity as jurors, we won't be able to absolve any defendant we find liable, even if he is contrite. Punish we must. The severity of that punishment, however, could be impacted by our religious backgrounds. Will those of us who are true believers go easy on the wrongdoers?

* * *

In the courtroom, Judge Mendez began with a conciliatory speech. "You'll be pleased to learn that you're getting a raise," he told the jury. I grinned proudly, because I was the one who had initiated this pay increase. A few days ago, I'd happened upon a handbook in Room 452 that stated: "If service extends beyond thirty days [which it did a long time ago], an additional six dollars per day per juror may be authorized."

I'd written Mendez a note, and now it appeared that my request was being granted. Six extra bucks wasn't much, I was willing to concede. But it was a triumph, nonetheless: At least I'd gotten the "system" to work in the jury's favor for a change.

"Jurors who remain until the end of the trial," the judge added, "will get a lifetime exemption from further service in New York County."

Having appeased us with minor boons, Judge Mendez addressed a thorny issue: the trial's protracted length. "At the beginning, the Court told you the trial would take three months to complete," he reminded us—as if we needed reminding of this broken promise. (I loved how the judge called himself "the Court," handily absolving himself of any personal responsibility.)

"We haven't been able to work a full three months because we've had to accommodate some members of the jury." (It's true, a few of us *have* needed time off; for example, we didn't meet the day Shawn had a job interview, or the day Aaron testified in one of his drug cases. Even so, the lawyers have taken days off, too, so don't blame us only! I thought.)

"Certain witnesses have taken a little longer than

necessary [my italics]," Mendez continued. Whoa, I thought: Did the judge just admit that the lawyers' examinations had taken an inordinate amount of time? "That is, longer than *expected*," Mendez corrected himself.

"Some things, we just have no control over," he explained. "So please bear with us. We're doing everything in our power to move this trial along. Don't take it out on the attorneys. They're simply representing their clients the best way they know how." Okay, I thought, I won't take it out on them. I'll take it out on you, judge. You're the boss. Can't you get your underlings in line?

* * *

When Mendez had finished his speech, the plaintiffs' attorneys began their next task: pinning liability on defendant Sorbara, the concrete subcontractor.

To my astonishment, Panzella had no questions for the company's first witness, Joseph Sorbara, who is Marino and Carmela Sorbara's son and was the superintendent for the Ninety-First Street project. It seemed unlikely that the ever-loquacious Panzella would voluntarily cede her turn, but the reason for her exclusion from direct examination remained hidden from us jurors.

Karten, one of the lawyers for the Kurtaj estate, seemed thrilled to have first dibs for a change. She went straight for the jugular: "Mr. Sorbara, have you ever explained to Mrs. Leo," Karten huffed, pointing to Don's bereaved mother in the audience, "why, even after the accident, your company still uses Mr. Lomma's cranes? Do you think that's honoring Don's memory?"

As forecasted in their opening statement (which, at this point, I barely remembered), the Kurtaj team blamed Sorbara for careless oversight of the crane that collapsed.

"Sir, did you know a crack had been discovered in this same crane on its previous job, also a Sorbara job?" Karten asked Sorbara.

"Yes," Sorbara replied.

"Did you check to make sure it had been properly repaired before you used it on Ninety-First Street?"

"All we could do was give it a surface inspection, you know, look it over visually."

That's right, I remembered: It was an undisputed fact that the alleged defect in the weld was *not* visible to the naked eye.

"But you could have hired a third party to do an internal inspection, right?" insisted Karten.

"Yes," conceded Sorbara, flashing a plaintive smile in the jury's direction.

I sympathized with Sorbara. His company's inaction seemed reasonable to me. I've never rented a crane, but the last time I rented a car, I didn't take it to the shop to have it checked out. Why should the Sorbara company spend its own money on *another* inspection, particularly when the crane had already supposedly been cleared by both Lomma and the City?

* * *

We've got next week off, because Kayla has to deejay a music cruise in the Caribbean. (Mendez evidently feels obliged to accommodate any trips we jurors had planned for *after* the trial's projected end date.) Hipster that she is, even Kayla's business junkets are super cool.

February 9

When Melanie lined us up to enter the courtroom this morning, we had to wait so long that we became increasingly punchy, like a bunch of restless kindergartners. Aisha blasted a tune on her smartphone and did a little dance. Some of the jurors joined in; others (including me) observed in amusement.

Tony turned to Sandra and said, "By the way, thanks for taking care of Oscar this weekend."

"Who's Oscar?" I asked.

"Tony's dog," replied Sandra.

"He's incontinent," added Tony, "so I had to teach Sandra how to change his diaper."

I carried with me into the courtroom the image of tough-cop Tony changing a doggy diaper.

* * *

When Joseph Sorbara retook the stand, Karten was suddenly as nice as pie. Did the Kurtaj estate settle with this defendant last week? I wondered. (Once again, we jurors got no elucidation from the judge or anyone else.)

In any case, it was clear that Karten had let Sorbara out of the doghouse. Now it was New York Crane, rather than the Sorbara company, that had failed to keep the crane in shipshape condition.

"Whose responsibility is it to do preventive maintenance on Lomma's cranes?" Karten asked Sorbara.

"Lomma's," Sorbara replied.

"But after he delivers a crane to a work site, according to the rental contract, whose responsibility is it to maintain it?"

"Ours. If something goes wrong while we're using one of Lomma's cranes, he charges us to fix it."

"So is there any incentive for Lomma to do preventive maintenance?"

"No, not really."

Sorbara was cross-examined by Fuerth's associate, Cruz Williams, who appears to be in her early thirties, probably the youngest lawyer in the courtroom. (Later, Melanie told me that Leo et al. v. Lomma et al. is, in fact, Williams's first trial.)

Williams is also the nicest-looking of all the attorneys, with olive skin, wide-set brown eyes, and high cheekbones. She favors tight-fitting jackets over short skirts, and high-heeled pumps that are at least a half-size too big, which make her look like a little girl playing dress-up. She heaved a binder onto the podium and addressed her questions with the same organized, pencil-checking methodology employed by Fuerth, her mentor (regarding the law, that is, *not* fashion).

Through her questioning, Williams tried to shift responsibility for the crane's safe upkeep away from Lomma and back on Sorbara. To do so, she asked Sorbara about a crane safety checklist that one of his employees was supposed to fill out but didn't.

"I object to this whole line of questioning," declared Slattery, Sorbara's attorney.

"Sustained," agreed the judge.

"I object to the speaking objection," Williams replied. (A "speaking objection" is one that includes more than a one- or two-word explanation,

Cruz Williams, a lawyer for defendant Lomma. *Courtroom Sketch by Juror Alison Colby.*

and it's not allowed because it could have an unduly negative influence on the jury.)

"I object to your objection," Slattery retorted.

"I object to *you*," interjected Fuerth, pointing at Slattery.

"No objection here!" exclaimed Karten, who was enjoying her opponents' ridiculous tit for tat.

Mendez glowered at all of them.

"My question is, as you sit here today," Williams resumed, "do you know if any Sorbara employee *actually* checked the safety switches on the crane that morning?"

"No, I don't know for sure," replied Sorbara.

Pleased by this answer, Williams made an exaggerated checkmark in her binder and smiled broadly. It was a rare victory for Lomma's team.

February 10

When it came to Brady Marine, the last party on the plaintiffs' hit list, their attorneys did another one-eighty (as they eventually had with Sorbara): Right out of the gate, they *defended* this defendant.

Perhaps, I thought, they've settled with, or even dropped the charges against, Brady Marine. That way, I reasoned, they could shift more blame for the allegedly defective weld onto a defendant with deeper pockets, Mr. Lomma. (I'm just speculating here; once again, no one bothered to explain to the jury why the plaintiffs were suddenly siding with a defendant. Besides, if my hypothesis were correct, why would Brady still have a seat at the table in this trial?)

In any case, I'd never understood how Brady Marine could possibly be liable for another company's (RTR's) allegedly poor workmanship.

O'Neill, one of the Kurtaj attorneys, cleared things up for me through his examination of Brady Marine's president, Daniel Muirhead.

Here's how O'Neill explained it. According to New York Crane, it had hired Brady to perform not one but *two* services: one, weld the RTR bearing to the bottom of the Kodiak crane's turntable; and two, test the Chinese-made weld in that bearing to make sure it was sound. It was the second task that had put Brady in hot water. Lomma claimed that Brady had neglected to test the Chinese weld, meaning Brady was, from Lomma's perspective, at least partly responsible for the accident.

"Here's the invoice you sent New York Crane for your work," said O'Neill, handing it to Muirhead. "In this line, it says 'Tested *all* [my italics] welds.' Which welds were you referring to, Mr. Muirhead?"

"The welds performed by Brady Marine," Muirhead replied unequivocally.

"Did anyone at New York Crane ask you to test the Chinese weld?"

"No."

"Do you *ever* test anyone else's welding?"

"Never. We test only our own welding."

"Did you even know there *was* a Chinese weld?"

"No. It wasn't visible."

When Williams cross-examined Muirhead, she insisted that the word "all" *did* include the Chinese weld, and that New York Crane had verbally asked Brady Marine to test it.

Muirhead retorted, "As I told Mr. O'Neill, Brady Marine *never* tests anyone else's welds, only our own." This claim made sense to me: Why on earth would Brady take on this extra responsibility? What's more, Williams had nothing in writing to prove that New York Crane had asked Brady to test the RTR weld.

Undeterred, Williams took a different tack.

"While your company performed its own welding, it might have damaged the RTR weld, right?" she asked Muirhead.

"No. My welder concentrated the heat of his instruments on his own work," he replied. "He's very experienced. I'd trust him with my life."

When Muirhead left the stand, I was convinced that his company had done nothing wrong. Then I wondered: If Lomma's theory is that operator error, not a defective weld, caused the accident, why was his team wasting all this time claiming it was someone else's fault that the weld was bad? Were they hedging their bets?

If that was the case, they were shooting themselves in the foot. If Fuerth and Williams didn't have complete confidence in their operator-error theory, why should the jury?

* * *

The plaintiffs' lawyers have finally finished the liability section of their case. Now it was time for them to address the issue of damages.

They'll try to prove that their clients are owed a king's ransom for the deaths of their loved ones.

FOUR

THE PLAINTIFFS' CASE: DAMAGES

This morning, I grabbed Bob before he rushed out the door to his *actual* job (unlike my pretend one).

"I think the plaintiffs are going to start the damages phase of the trial today," I told him. "I know damages are monetary compensation, but can you explain the different types to me?"

"I've got to make it quick," he replied, glancing at his watch. "One category is called economic damages: These compensate the plaintiffs for the financial support they would have received from their loved ones had they not died.

"The other category is called noneconomic damages," Bob continued. "These compensate the plaintiffs for the mental and physical distress their loved ones experienced just before they died."

"Okay, I've got it. Thanks," I replied.

Who will get the damages in this trial? Don Leo didn't have a will, so they'll be shared by the estate of his father, who died in 2011, and his mother, Maria Leo. (Don's parents were divorced.) Ramadan Kurtaj didn't have a will, either, but I'm not yet sure which of his relatives are his beneficiaries.

* * *

In the courtroom, plaintiff Leo, as usual, went first. Panzella started with the issue of economic damages. She didn't even try to convince the jury that Don had ever provided for his father. This would have been a hard sell: Before he died, Don's dad not only earned a good living as a tower crane operator, but he also drew a pension as a former firefighter.

Panzella *did* claim, however, that Don supported his mother, helping with upkeep of the Staten Island home in which he and his siblings had been raised, and giving her money when she hit hard times.

When Maria Leo took the stand, I thought: I bet she's about my age. (I was right: Maria is fifty-four). Attractive in an everywoman way, with the brown hair and eyes of her deceased son, Maria testified, "Don was devoted to me. When my husband and I divorced, Don wanted to do the things that a man about the house would do. I didn't even have to ask." He planted shrubs, painted the bedrooms, shoveled snow, and cleaned the gutters. Plus, claimed Maria, Don paid out of his own pocket for any supplies he needed for these home-maintenance projects.

"Don was always giving me presents," Maria added. "In fact, I'm wearing the diamond earrings he bought me after he began earning two hundred to two hundred and fifty thousand dollars a year as a tower crane operator," she added proudly. (I didn't realize he made *that* much: not bad for blue-collar work.)

When Maria got in trouble financially—she had decided to downsize, selling her house and buying an apartment, but the house sale fell through and she was stuck with two mortgages—Maria said Don told her, " 'Don't worry, Ma, I'll help you out.' I'm embarrassed to admit it," Maria confessed. "Don gave me five hundred to fifteen hundred dollars a month.

"Don even wanted to buy my house from me—"

Panzella interrupted her. "Remember, you're not allowed to tell the jury about that."

"Sorry," Maria replied.

Why didn't the defendants object to this slip—the claim that Don would have paid Maria however many hundreds of thousands of dollars her home was worth had he not died? I guess they didn't want to look like they were harassing a bereaved mother.

"Don assured me he would take care of me in my old age," Maria continued. "You know, I didn't ask him to sign anything to that effect. I had no idea I'd be sitting here having to prove it to all of you."

At this point, Panzella played the sympathy card: She asked Maria to revisit the day of the accident. Maria immediately teared up and reached for the tissue box someone had thoughtfully placed on the witness stand. "When my ex-husband called me at my office that morning, I was surprised. I hadn't heard from him in ages. He sounded frantic. 'Did you hear there was a crane collapse?' he said. At first, I thought, 'Why are you telling me this?' Then it hit me. It's my son. He said, 'You have to get here fast.'

"I called Don, and he didn't pick up. Then I got my pocketbook, and I ran out of my office. I got downstairs, and I was still calling my son because I didn't know exactly where to go." Then Maria's ex-husband called again to ask if she'd left yet. " 'Yes, but where am I going?' I pleaded."

"Ninety-First and First. Hurry!"

When Maria got there, her world was shattered. Her beloved firstborn child was dead.

"I don't have any more questions," Panzella declared with dramatic solemnity. "It's enough."

The judge asked Maria if she needed a break, and she gratefully accepted.

February 13

"Pack it up," Melanie commanded us jurors this morning.

The trial is over, I thought. The plaintiffs settled, and we're going home. What a letdown.

But then our court officer added, as if it were of little consequence, "You're moving to a different courtroom and a different jury room."

Phew! These past four and a half months haven't been a waste. My "purpose" hasn't come to a premature end.

Melanie was about to close the door when I made a dash for the ever-present Halloween pumpkin. I grabbed it by its stem and the gourd spontaneously combusted, like a plant version of Crook, the junk merchant who met a similar end in the Dickens novel *Bleak House.* (I know, I've referred to this nineteenth-century writer before; but it turns out his novels are particularly pertinent to this trial.)

The pumpkin had looked perfectly fine on the outside, possibly preserved by the chill of the barely heated room. But its innards had become a rotten mound of gray, dusty flesh, parts of which swirled in the air like a ghost. I was gobsmacked by the gourd's dramatic demise and the aptness of the image it conveyed, a character in a book about a legal proceeding that also goes in circles and never ends.

Our new courtroom, Room 442, differs from our old one in two ways: It's smaller, and its setup is reversed. In Room 300, the jury box was to the judge's left and the lawyers' right, but in this one, it's the opposite. Karten, the attorney who spends the most time peering at us jurors to gauge our reactions, seemed discombobulated by this change, and kept turning her eagle eye to her right instead of her left. Otherwise, Room 442 was much the same— high-ceilinged, leaky-windowed, and punishingly-chilled.

* * *

When Maria Leo retook the stand, Fuerth abdicated the dirty work of cross-examining the bereaved mother to Williams.

"I want to begin by offering my condolences. I am very—" Williams began.

Maria stiffened. "Please don't go there."

"I am very sorry—" Williams tried again.

"Please," repeated Maria.

"—for your loss," finished Williams.

"For seven years you have been blaming my son for the accident. How can you even—" Maria growled.

"I understand this is—" Williams tried again.

"Skip it," Maria interjected.

"—difficult for you," continued Williams.

"Please skip it."

"I am going to try to make this—" Williams kept at it.

Panzella stepped in. "Is there a question, your Honor?"

"Judge, this is just common courtesy," intoned Fuerth, defending his associate's attempt to play nice.

"Please continue, Ms. Williams," Mendez told her.

Williams's job was to counter the narrative that Don supported his mother and would have continued to support her until she died, thereby reducing the damages that Lomma and his businesses will owe if they're found liable.

"Did you understand that once Mr. Leo and his fiancée got married, that the two of them would be supporting each other?" Williams asked.

"Of course," replied Maria indignantly. "But not at the expense of Don disowning his own mother."

Williams told Maria that Don's fiancée had said, in her deposition, that she was unaware of Don supporting anyone else financially. Maria retorted, "My son would never have embarrassed me by telling his fiancée that he was giving his mother money." Williams added that in her own deposition, when asked if Don gave her money, Maria had replied in the negative. "You didn't ask me about cash, which he *did* give me. You asked about checks, and affidavits, and stuff like that, and I got nervous. I didn't want to expose my vulnerability, my reliance on my son."

Maria's rationalization rang hollow to me.

February 16

This morning, we jurors finished our third jigsaw puzzle, which depicted another complicated, post-Impressionist painting.

As I admired our handiwork, I realized that this trial is like a puzzle, or perhaps I should say, two puzzles. The resulting "picture"—a crane collapse that killed two people—will be the same, but its construction will vary. One puzzle's pieces are being shaped by the plaintiffs, to represent their version of the truth behind the picture, while the second puzzle's pieces, once the defendants present their case, will be cut into different shapes, outlining an alternate truth.

These two pictures of the truth were, of course, painted in the lawyers' opening statements. But they were presented so long ago that it's become very difficult to conjure them in our minds so that the jurors have something to refer to as we try to put the pieces together.

What's more, we jurors don't get to choose the pieces ourselves. They're picked out and handed to us by the lawyers, often in a peculiar order, and some are missing—withheld by the judge or deemed unimportant by the attorneys—while others don't seem to fit anywhere. Case in point: All that evidence about the logistics of Lomma's various businesses. Where does that piece fit?

Anyway, we're not supposed to put the pieces together until the end, when we deliberate. But why can't we get started? We're allowed to study each separate piece, but there our assessment must end? That's like allowing two people to date—to assess the pieces of each other's personality—but not to consider whether these pieces might fit together to form a marriage.

* * *

Speaking of marriage, today we heard from Janine Belcastro, Don's fiancée. Why did Panzella ask her to testify? I wondered. She wasn't yet married to Don, so she won't get a penny from this proceeding. Maybe Panzella put her on the stand to drum up yet more sympathy for her client. If that was her goal, Panzella achieved it big-time.

Janine was the nicest-looking witness so far. Tall and slender, with long, blond hair, her blue-green eyes welled up as soon as she took the stand.

"Tell us about Don," Panzella began.

"He was like a big kid," Janine replied. "He had a lot of exuberance for life and a passion for lots of different things."

Janine, a social worker (read: a good person), met Don on the Jersey shore in 2002. They bought a home together, got engaged in 2007, and set their wedding date for June 21, 2008. "We'd been together for a long time, and we wanted to start a family," said Janine, gazing through one of the courtroom's oversized windows, "so we wanted to get married as soon as possible."

Panzella showed us several photos of the happy couple, including one with Don's extended family that included the suntanned blonde who often accompanies Maria to court. It turns out that she's Don's aunt, and she lives in the same condominium complex on the Jersey shore as Janine. (After Don died, his parents paid off Don's half of the mortgage so Janine could keep the home for herself.)

Three weeks before the wedding, Janine was at work, sitting at her desk doodling table arrangements for the reception, when her mother called.

" 'Don is on the Upper East Side, his crane, there's been an accident!' " she told her unsuspecting daughter.

Someone sent a car to pick up Janine. "I didn't know where I was going," Janine explained, looking up in an attempt to keep her mounting tears from running down her face. "When I got there, I knew it wasn't a hospital. It was a medical examiner's office. Don's whole family was waiting outside. I got out of the car, and they were hugging me and saying 'I'm so sorry.' "

Everyone in the jury box teared up, and even the attorneys on the defense's side of the table looked misty-eyed.

* * *

After we were dismissed for the day, I found Guy surrounded by a pack of lawyers outside our new courtroom. I caught his eye and gave him a questioning look. "You're not allowed to talk to the attorneys. What on earth is going on?" I wished I could ask.

When I exited the subway, I texted Guy, and he replied that he had been excused from the jury because he got a promotion at work and needs to return full-time. Apparently, after Guy was set free, the lawyers were at liberty to talk to him, and they peppered him with questions about his impressions of the trial thus far.

"I can't believe they're allowed to do that," I texted back. "Seems like cheating. Anyway, what did you say?"

"I can't tell you," he replied. "I promised the judge I wouldn't talk about it."

"Who's going to keep me entertained now that you're leaving?" I pleaded.

I'm going to miss my jury husband.

February 17

In the jury room this morning, Martha's head was buried in her *New York Times*. Shawn turned the pages of his *New York Daily News* indifferently, while his usual pastry and coffee sat untouched. Erin looked up from her book and sighed. Alison stared at her laptop vacantly and took occasional bites of the hard-boiled eggs she purchases from the food cart outside the courthouse. Aisha rummaged through the candy bowls that have magically been replenished ever since Halloween, but found nothing to her liking. Everyone else scrolled mechanically through their phones.

I tried to catch someone's eye, to make communication,

but there were no takers. Even Tony, who can usually be counted on for an amusing back-and-forth, had his head down. With the trial in its fifth month, the prevailing mood in the jury room has become one of grumpy resignation.

* * *

It was a good day for a compelling witness, and we got one: Ramadan Kurtaj's father. His testimony, like Maria Leo's, concerned the issue of economic damages.

Uke (pronounced OO-key) Kurtaj, a seventy-one-year-old sheep farmer, entered the courtroom haltingly. He gazed at the courtroom's assorted inhabitants with a look of bewildered awe. His balding scalp was framed by a circle of grizzled hair, and his handsome, weather-wrinkled face was adorned with a mustache ironically similar to that of Tibor Varganyi, Lomma's former mechanic. Uke wore a heavy wool suit whose purpose seemed practical—to provide warmth—rather than decorative. Under his jacket peeked a waistcoat containing a pocket watch at the end of a gold chain, likely a prized possession.

Ramadan's father looked like he'd been transported here from a bygone era.

Uke doesn't speak English, so he was accompanied by an Albanian interpreter. Now a father of nine, seven boys and two girls, Uke told us that he made the long trip from the Eastern European country of Kosovo to New York with his son Halil, who sat in the gallery next to Uke's niece, Jev Sinanaj (pronounced SI-nan-edge). Jev has lived in New York City for many years and speaks fluent English, so

Ramadan's parents asked her to represent them as co-administratrix—the other one being Ramadan's widow, Selvi Sinanovic—of their deceased son's estate.

Now it was clear who Ramadan's beneficiaries were. But it was a puzzling arrangement: Under American law, since Ramadan died without a will, his widow should inherit his estate in its entirety, including any damages we award. But for some reason (as usual, we jurors have been left in the dark), Selvi was sharing it with Ramadan's parents.

In fact, this split is the reason why the Kurtaj estate has two principal attorneys. I finally figured out that Karten and O'Neill are only "sort of" working together: Karten represents just Ramadan's parents, and O'Neill's client is his widow.

Because of this division of labor, Karten, rather than O'Neill, was the attorney who examined Uke. Her first order of business: to prove that Ramadan supported his parents, and would have continued to do so had he not died.

Before Karten began, Uke pulled a creased photo of Ramadan out of his pocket, which his lawyer showed the jury. Smiling proudly, Ramadan resembled his father, with blue eyes, a wide smile, and a muscular build.

While we passed the picture around, Uke gave us a mini–history lesson about Kosovo—a lesson that would illustrate why Uke so desperately needed his son Ramadan's financial help.

After the country of Yugoslavia broke up, Uke explained, Kosovo became a province of the nation of Serbia. "When

Christian Serbs attacked and even killed Muslims like us," Uke testified, "we had to flee our home with nothing but the clothes on our backs. My family walked one hundred and fifty miles to Albania, where we settled in a refugee camp."

Deceased plaintiff Ramadan Kurtaj. *Sketch by Juror Alison Colby.*

When the Kurtajs returned to their village after Kosovo won the war for its independence (a year-long battle in which eighteen-year-old Ramadan volunteered to serve), "we had to rebuild our home because it had been burned to the ground," Uke told us. He and some of his sons, including Ramadan, then started a construction business to take advantage of the post-war building demand; but once work dried up, they returned to subsistence farming.

* * *

We broke for lunch, and after we returned to the jury room, we heard sirens blaring outside. Melanie entered to inform us that the trial wouldn't start up again for at least another hour.

Kayla asked, "What's going on?"

"A couple of people in the courtroom are unwell," Melanie replied before dashing out.

"Do you think Fuerth and Panzella got into a fist fight?" one of the jurors joked.[1]

A few minutes later, Melanie escorted us into an emptied courtroom. Judge Mendez entered and, without explanation, dismissed us for the day.

February 19

I couldn't wait to get back this morning to find out what the crisis in the courtroom had been.

Apparently, Ramadan's father, Uke Kurtaj, had become so distressed when he recognized the defense attorney who had taken his deposition that he had heart palpitations. Concerned about her elderly client's health, Karten called an ambulance. Then Karten laid into this lawyer for making her client sick, which made him feel ill as well. Another

---

[1] After the trial was over, O'Neill told me that an opposing attorney on a different case once punched Panzella so hard that he broke her nose. This remark was not as absurd as it seemed.

defense lawyer called a second ambulance, this one for his ailing colleague.

Thankfully, both parties were now feeling fine.

* * *

After we entered the courtroom, I scanned the faces of the defense lawyers, wondering which one had been so mean to the aging, defenseless sheep farmer. Unfortunately, there were no discernible clues.

Looking none the worse for wear, Ramadan's father continued his testimony. After Ramadan married Selvi Sinanovic (an American citizen whose parents had immigrated to the U.S. from the Eastern European country of Montenegro), Uke explained, Ramadan moved into his bride's family home in the Bronx. "As soon as my son found a job, he began sending money home," Uke declared forthrightly, exhibiting none of the shame to which Maria Leo had confessed when her son helped her out.

Uke did not have a bank account while Ramadan was alive, so he had no financial records to prove the cash payments he claimed his son had given him. But since they were not outlandish (a total of eleven thousand dollars over a two-year period), they seemed believable to me. Uke showed us the envelope that contained the money his son gave him just weeks before he died: On it, Ramadan had written, "I greet all of you wholeheartedly, and I send you all my best from America." Ramadan added the following salutation: "Tung!", which, ironically, means "Live long!"

"How did Ramadan's death affect you?" asked Karten.

Uke pulled a cloth handkerchief out of his breast pocket, wiped his eyes, and replied with solemn dignity, "When a brother of yours dies, it's like losing an arm. When a child of yours is dead, you have lost your heart."

February 20

"Growing up, I wasn't allowed to have any kind of life. It was home, school, home, school, period," declared Selvi Sinanovic self-pityingly when she took the stand this morning.

This is how Ramadan's widow began her life's story. A tale whose ultimate purpose, like Maria's and Uke's, was a practical one: to demonstrate the economic support the deceased provided her.

With shoulder-length, henna-red hair, and flawlessly made-up brown eyes, Selvi wore all black, either to emphasize her widowhood, or to camouflage her stout frame. Selvi's attorney, O'Neill, who has spent much of the trial slumped in his seat while displaying a sardonic grin like that of Lewis Carroll's Cheshire cat, transformed into a kindly father figure when his client took the stand. "Take a deep breath," he told Selvi. "You'll be fine."

Born in 1987, a year after her parents moved to the U.S., Selvi claimed her father was not only strict and controlling, but also "verbally and physically abusive." I thought O'Neill might ask Selvi to elaborate, to play the sympathy card, but he resisted this tactic.

Instead, O'Neill asked Selvi to explain how she met Ramadan. When she was about twelve years old, Selvi told us, her family started making annual trips to Kosovo to visit relatives, including the Kurtajs (to whom they were already related by marriage). As she got older, Selvi claimed, "Ramadan and I clicked. And my father was like, 'This is the guy for you. This is my son,' and he was so excited." While on spring break from her senior year of high school, eighteen-year-old Selvi married Ramadan.

Once he arrived in New York, Ramadan immediately found a well-paying construction job. "In Albanian families, a son supports his parents, and the economy was really bad in Kosovo, so Ramadan sent money home, as much as he could," Selvi claimed, corroborating Uke's account. "He was generous with everybody, with his friends, with his family, with me."

The following year, Selvi became pregnant—by another man, the result of a one-night stand. "My father banished me. None of my family was allowed to see me, not even Ramadan." Several jurors shook their heads, whether shocked by the infidelity, the ostracism, or both, I couldn't tell.

"I moved in with a friend who lived in Maryland," Selvi told us. "Ramadan and I met in secret, even after my daughter was born. He continued to support me, giving me about three hundred dollars a month.

"I know Ramadan had been hurt by the situation," Selvi admitted, "but he forgave me. Ramadan was hoping to convince my father to end the banishment. We wanted to get back together. I loved him with all my heart."

* * *

I rewound scenes from this international soap opera on the subway ride home. Seemed like a marriage of convenience to me, despite Selvi's claim that it was a marriage of love.

March 2

I thought I'd get kicked off the jury today.

Over the weekend, while telling Bob a story about the trial that we had agreed was above board, I let slip the name of the law firm representing one of the defendants. "My company uses them," Bob said, rubbing his forehead. "I'll have to tell my contact there that you're a juror on this trial. He'll tell the judge, who will tell the attorneys. The plaintiffs' lawyers will argue that you'll be biased in favor of this firm's defendant because of my relationship. You might be dismissed."

"What? That's ridiculous!" I exclaimed. "I couldn't care less what law firm you guys use."

"I know, but they may not see it that way," Bob replied.

* * *

Will I be let go at the beginning or the end of the day? I wondered when I got to the jury room. I was escorted into the courtroom along with the others, and nobody gave me a funny look. They probably don't know yet, I thought as I sat on the edge of my seat.

Ramadan's widow retook the stand, to be cross-examined by Williams, who would try to refute Selvi's claim that her husband supported her and would have continued to do so had he not died. Williams proved that Selvi had no evidence that Ramadan ever gave her money, either before *or* after the banishment.

"Do you have any letters, any cell phone records, any documentation whatsoever of your communications with Ramadan after you moved to Maryland?" asked Williams.

"Why would I have to document my communications with my husband?" Selvi replied defensively. "I didn't know he would be killed."

After her daughter was born, Selvi told Williams, she applied for housing assistance. "Did you write on the application that you were receiving three hundred dollars a month from Mr. Kurtaj?" asked Williams.

"No," muttered Selvi, staring at the ceiling. Maybe because she wasn't, I thought, or maybe because she was, but kept quiet because it would reduce her chances of getting government aid. In any case, Selvi claimed, "I didn't tell *anyone* that Ramadan was giving me money until *after* the accident, when I told just my mom."

When Williams asked Selvi about Ramadan's job, she replied, "I don't know how much money he made, or whether he had medical, dental, or life insurance."

"Did you ever learn, during that period that you say the two of you were planning on reconciling," Williams continued, "that Mr. Kurtaj had named his cousin Jev as the beneficiary of his life insurance policy?"

"No. I just said, I didn't know anything about all that stuff," Selvi retorted.

"When did you find out that Ramadan had died?"

"On the day of the accident."

"In your deposition, you said you didn't find out until two days later, when one of the few relatives who secretly kept in touch with you just happened to call."

"I don't remember that."

Selvi did not go to Ramadan's memorial service in New York, or to his funeral in Kosovo. "I had wanted to go," claimed Selvi, "but I couldn't because of the banishment," which, she told us, her father finally ended a couple of years ago.

When Williams ended her examination, I thought: Even if the marriage was a sham, and Ramadan never gave Selvi a penny, so what? As Ramadan's spouse, Selvi is legally entitled to her inheritance.

* * *

Back in the jury room, we couldn't help but trade opinions on Selvi's plight. (I'm coming clean: I've started discussing the case with the other jurors.)

"That poor child!" exclaimed Martha. "She was essentially sold to another family."

"Selvi's situation is so pitiful," I added.

Aaron (who, as a divorcé, may have been channeling bitter feelings) was less sympathetic. "Selvi doesn't deserve a penny," he countered.

"I agree," said Aisha scornfully. Her reaction surprised me: I'd have thought Aisha would sympathize with Selvi, a fellow teenaged—and now single—mom. (I considered asking Aisha why she was antagonistic to Selvi, but decided that would be prying.)

As we packed up, I worried that Melanie would tell me that the judge wanted to see me before I left. That I'd be summarily dismissed because of Bob's connection to the firm representing one of the defendants.

Thank goodness it didn't happen.

March 3

"Ramadan and I *never* talked about Selvi," claimed Jev Sinanaj, the co-administratrix of the Kurtaj estate, when she took the stand this morning.

As the representative of Ramadan's parents, Jev's job was to downplay his widow's importance, thereby reducing Selvi's share of any damages we may award Ramadan's estate. Jev's testimony should create considerable tension between her attorney, Karten, and Selvi's lawyer, O'Neill, I thought. But when I stole a look at O'Neill, he was his usual slumped self, seemingly unperturbed by Jev's dismissive comments about his client.

Tall and voluptuous, with long, black hair and a heavily made-up face, thirty-something Jev confirmed that Ramadan gave his parents—but not Selvi—money whenever he could, just as she provides for her own parents back in Kosovo. "That's something we do in our culture, we sacrifice for our families," Jev proclaimed proudly. Then she scowled at the jury, as if she'd like to add, "Unlike you selfish Americans, who neglect your parents once you no longer need them."

When Jev found out about Ramadan's accident, she was the first of his relatives to get to the hospital. "I had hoped to know what Ramadan's last wishes were, but I never saw him alive again." At the end of Karten's examination, Jev added, "It's difficult to go on with our lives without Ramadan. And this process [the criminal and civil trials] going on for seven years, it makes everything harder on us. Ramadan will be in our hearts forever. May his soul rest in peace."

Curiously, even though Jev's testimony damaged Selvi's case, O'Neill passed on direct examination. "Why isn't he sticking up for his client?" I wrote in my notebook.

I guess there must be some behind-the-scenes arrangement between O'Neill and Karten. Perhaps they're concerned that we jurors could be so put off by infighting between them that we might penalize them *both* by minimizing the total amount of any potential award.

How will they end up splitting the money? I wondered.

March 19

"Did you enjoy your time back on the beat?" I heard Tony ask Aaron. (We'd had more time off because the lawyers had needed to discuss several case-related issues outside the jury's presence.)

"I'm exhausted," replied Aaron. "I like my juror hours a lot better than my cop hours!"

Tony laughed. "Same here, man."

* * *

Now that the plaintiffs' attorneys have elicited testimony about the economic support Don and Ramadan would have provided their relatives had they not been killed, it was time for them to address noneconomic damages. The law divides this type of award into two categories, both of which Dr. Howard Schwartz, a witness for the plaintiffs, addressed in his testimony today.

One kind of noneconomic damages, explained Schwartz, a forensic medicine specialist, is called "pre-impact terror." In the case of Don and Ramadan, this was the *emotional* distress that they experienced as the crane was collapsing. The other kind, called "pain and suffering," was the *physical* anguish they endured from the moment they were injured to the moment they died.

"Why are the survivors compensated for someone *else's* distress—the decedents'—but not their *own* anguish at losing their loved ones?" I wrote in my notebook. A few attorneys had asked some potential jurors, during *voir dire,* if they were bothered by this type of redress. But they hadn't asked me, and I hadn't given the issue any thought until now.

Then I started wondering why the law divides this distress into two categories, one pre-injury, and the other post-injury.

To my mind, the only legitimate reason to distinguish the two would be if the experts—doctors, psychologists, philosophers, the clergy, or members of some other discipline—believe fear is worse than pain (or vice versa), and that one is worth more money than the other. Otherwise, why not put them both in a category called "really bad feelings" and leave it at that? What's more, wouldn't the two sensations overlap?

Come to think of it, why compensate for these feelings in the first place? What legal luminary of ages past, I wondered, devised this peculiar system of recompense? It would make more sense, I think, to compensate for deprivation of life. Admittedly, this would also be hard to valuate, but at least it seems worthier of valuation than "fear" and "pain" are.

I'd expected the inner workings of the justice system to be obscure, but I hadn't expected them to be weird.

Too late for doubts now. When I was sworn in by the judge, I pledged to follow the law, whether or not I agreed with it.

* * *

Dr. Schwartz addressed Don Leo's damages first. He

described not only the type of injuries Don experienced, but also his level of fear and pain, as well as the length of time that Don suffered. (The details of Don's demise were so grisly that Panzella suggested his mother, Maria, leave the courtroom.)

First, Don's injuries: The worst—the immediate cause of death—was "blunt impact craniocervical trauma," which means the spinal cord was severed from the brain. In fact, virtually every part of Don's body was broken. On his torso, he had fractures of the ribs and pelvis; lung, liver, and spleen lacerations; and hemorrhaging kidneys. On his extremities, his upper-arm, shin, and calf bones were fractured. In a rare display of restraint, Panzella announced that she would not show us Don's autopsy photos.

As Schwartz began describing the sequence of these injuries, several defense attorneys objected, and after a brief sidebar in our presence, Melanie removed the jury from the courtroom. The order in which Don's injuries occurred is a hot-button issue, because any one of them could also determine when Don lost consciousness, and thus was no longer able to feel fear, pain, or suffering.

Upon our return, Schwartz was permitted to describe this sequence despite the defense's previous protestations. "Don's arm and leg fractures were likely caused when he *consciously* braced himself against the sides of the crane cab as it started to fall," he claimed. "He was trying to protect himself from further harm." Don's torso injuries weren't fatal either, said Schwartz, but, like the arm and leg fractures, they were extremely painful.

As for Don's pre-impact terror, it too would have been severe. "The crane was no longer under his control, and he was experiencing panic, frustration, and severe anxiety," Schwartz testified. "His body was starting to sweat, his heart was racing, and his fear was overwhelming."

Don would have continued to suffer, this expert claimed, until the crane hit the street, at which point Don finally lost consciousness, was virtually decapitated, and died. In other words, according to Schwartz, Don experienced fear, as well as pain and suffering, during the *entire* time it took the crane to fall.

Schwartz didn't indicate which type of distress—emotional or physical—was worse, or which Don felt more of. He also didn't convince me that Don was still alive when the cab collided with the ground. But Schwartz did leave me with the impression that Don's death was truly dreadful.

In his cross-examination, Fuerth made three important points regarding the length of time Don suffered: the time on the death certificate, 8:22 a.m., was when it was signed, *not* when Don died; since Don wasn't wearing a hard hat or a seatbelt[2], he could have been knocked unconscious when the cab struck the building across the street, and some of his arm and leg injuries could have occurred at that point, too; and the structural engineer who had testified for the *plaintiffs* had claimed that the entire collapse lasted just fifteen to twenty-five seconds.

---

2 Crane operators are not required to wear either a hard hat or a seatbelt when they're in the cab.

"So, twenty-five seconds would be the maximum amount of fear that Mr. Leo sustained, as well as the maximum duration of his pain and suffering, correct?" Fuerth asked Schwartz.

"Not necessarily, no," replied Schwartz unconvincingly.

* * *

After Schwartz left the stand, Panzella announced hostilely, "Your Honor, based on the Court's ruling of earlier today, I have no further witnesses."

It struck me as odd that Panzella had never put anyone on the stand to testify about Don's lost earning potential. (Perhaps the ruling to which Panzella alluded precluded her from doing so.) But I *was* relieved. With Panzella finished, I thought, perhaps the case will speed up.

March 20

Schwartz retook the stand today, this time to testify about Ramadan's injuries, as well as the length of time he experienced fear and pain.

Here's an accounting of Ramadan's horrific wounds: fractures of the skull, spine, right leg (which later had to be amputated), and right wrist; bleeding in the skull; crush injuries on the upper torso and chest; and lung contusions.

Schwartz addressed Ramadan's pre-impact terror first. "Ramadan saw the crane falling and yelled to his coworkers to get out of the way. He was very much aware that he might die or be seriously injured," said the doctor. "Like

Don, Ramadan would have been sweating, and his heart would have been racing."

Once he was pinned under the crane cab, Ramadan suffered incredible agony. "In medicine, we have a pain scale of one to ten. This magnitude of pain would have been much greater than ten. It would have been off the chart," Schwartz claimed.

Had Ramadan been wearing a helmet? I wondered. No one said. Since Ramadan, unlike Don, *was* out in the open, he should have been. If he wasn't, that could potentially benefit the defense. They could claim that by forgoing a helmet, Ramadan was partially responsible for his injuries. But no helmet could protect him from a seventy-five-ton crane cab, I reasoned, so maybe that's why this issue was never raised.

In any case, it took almost twenty minutes for emergency workers to extricate Ramadan from beneath the cab. Once in the ambulance, Ramadan was moaning, according to the ambulance attendant's notes. "This indicates that he was conscious and still feeling pain," the doctor explained. "The EMT also noted that Ramadan's pupils were reactive, proof that he had brain function, and he wasn't given a sedative or painkiller in the ambulance."

In the emergency room, Ramadan was administered a paralytic drug at 8:36 a.m., to keep him from moving and further injuring himself. "Ramadan was still aware of what was going on," this witness claimed, "but the paralytic prevented him from communicating his feelings."

Schwartz concluded that Ramadan suffered for *at least* thirty-six minutes before he hemorrhaged to death, during surgery to relieve the pressure in his abdominal cavity, at 12:14 p.m.

In her redirect examination, Karten added that at 10:50 a.m., it was reported that Ramadan's consciousness level had increased. "This means," says Schwartz, "that Ramadan was getting better and could have been feeling pain again." But in his re-cross, Fuerth, who had accused Schwartz of a thirty-year history of biased testimony in favor of plaintiffs, and mocked the doctor's claim that Ramadan's pain was "off the chart," deemed this notation a mistake.

"The operating room physician, who believed the note had been written by an intern, said it was incorrect," Fuerth told Schwartz.

"I don't happen to recall that," the doctor replied.

"I figured you wouldn't," said Fuerth sarcastically, an extraneous comment to which O'Neill objected vehemently.

* * *

After Schwartz left the stand, Karten put on a forensic accountant who testified about Ramadan's lost earning potential. This expert suggested we give Ramadan's parents two million dollars in economic damages, and five and a quarter million to Selvi.

Then Karten declared, "Your Honor, we rest our case."

These words were music to my ears.

It was *finally* the defense's turn.

FIVE

THE DEFENDANTS' CASE: LIABILITY

March 26

As we gathered in the jury room this morning, the seemingly cool, calm, and collected Kayla lost it.

"I just [gasp] can't [sob] do it [gulp] anymore," she exclaimed, while she shook, and the color rushed from her face.

The strain of jury duty, plus two jobs, had pushed Kayla over the edge.

She was having a panic attack.

One of the jurors rushed out of the room to get help, and returned with Melanie, who was taking no chances.

"I'm calling an ambulance," she declared.

"No, don't do that. I'll [choke] be okay," replied Kayla.

Unsure how to proceed, Melanie summoned Judge Mendez. He looks so much less imposing in our dinky jury room, I thought, than he does in the courtroom. If it weren't for the robe, he'd look like a regular person.

Mendez asked the rest of the jurors to leave the room.

After a few minutes, the judge exited. "Alternate Number Two's doing better," he said. "She just needs to rest a while longer. Please wait out here." After about ten minutes, Kayla opened the jury room door. "I'm ready now," she muttered to Melanie. We ambled into the courtroom as if it were just business as usual.

* * *

It was finally the defense lawyers' turn to present their case, and they started with the issue of liability. Fuerth, who went first, had placed an enormous demonstrative aid, several feet tall, on the far side of the courtroom, covered by a white sheet. He gave it a proud smile as he bounded to the podium.

"Good morning, ladies and gentlemen!" Fuerth exclaimed. I noted a new zing behind his knee-jerk salutation.

Panzella interrupted, "Your Honor, I have a matter I need to discuss."

"Come up," sighed the judge, removing his glasses to rub his eyes.

Fuerth deflated.

While the lawyers huddled, I peered at the yet-to-be-revealed show-and-tell in the corner with intense curiosity.

Would this mystery object be Lomma's golden ticket, I wondered?

* * *

As the sidebar got longer and louder, the judge asked Melanie to take us out. We remained in our jury room for almost an hour. Aaron, Tony, and Martha started another poker game, and Kayla lay her head on the table, happy to have the chance to calm her nerves. "I wish my boss would give me a raise," Aisha complained to Sandra. "He's so stingy." He's probably unhappy, I thought, that Aisha has been able to work only on Wednesdays and weekends for the past six months.

Come to think of it, I have no idea how Aisha supports herself and her children on three days of store-clerk wages and four days of jury-duty pay.

What about the others? Tony (who has no children, and whose wife is an attorney) and Aaron (who has a young son from his previous marriage, and who lives with his paralegal fiancée) are still getting regular pay from their employers, as are the single, childless Kayla and Alison. I believe Erin's employer stopped paying her recently, but she lives with her boyfriend, who has a well-paying job and who, I assume, won't let her starve.

Martha (who has no children and is married to a college professor) is retired, and I wasn't working, so our financial situations haven't changed, either. Sandra hasn't had much time for her fashion accessories business, but I don't know to what extent she depends on it financially. (Sandra's husband has his own business, and they have no children to support, so I assume she's okay.)

That leaves the single, childless Shawn, who used to work for the volunteer agency Americorps (which suggests that he, too, will favor the little guys in this trial), but is now "between jobs." His ability to subsist, like Aisha's, remains a mystery.

* * *

Melanie told us to take a long lunch break. When we returned, we entered the courtroom only to be dismissed for the day. Mendez also told us not to come back until Monday.

We heard no testimony at all today. At this rate, we'll be here forever.

March 30

Kayla didn't show up this morning. Three jurors down, nine to go. My new title is "Alternate Number One." I'm tantalizingly close to a seat in the room where it will happen.

* * *

When we entered the courtroom, Fuerth's much-anticipated demonstrative aid had disappeared.

Fuerth glared at the vacant spot where his show-and-tell had stood before calling his first witness, Ed Cox, to the stand. Cox's job would be to convince the jury that the Chinese weld did *not* cause the accident. This, in turn, would mean that Fuerth's clients, Lomma and his businesses, did not put a defective bearing in the crane; that they did not cause the accident; and that they are not liable.

With a long, shaggy, white beard, the sixty-something-year-old Cox wore khakis attached to his skinny frame by a worn belt, a strikingly ugly orange tie, and sneakers. (I'm no fashionista, but I think the lawyers should screen their witnesses' attire a little more carefully.)

A forensic engineer from Texas, Fuerth's expert witness began with an overview of his bona fides. "I wrote both my master's and doctoral theses on the subject of welding," Cox announced proudly, stroking his facial hair methodically.

The crux of Cox's defense was that the RTR weld, while flawed, was more than adequate. "We live in a world of imperfect welds," he told us. (There's a statement I never expected to hear in my life.) "Rarely do you find a perfect one, and when you do, it's in the aerospace industry. In construction," Cox continued, "most welds have flaws. You need to know how detrimental those flaws are, under what conditions those flaws remain benign, and under what conditions those flaws could have a negative effect."

As for the kind of weld you need in a crane bearing, Cox argued, it's perfectly fine if it contains minor defects, as did the one manufactured by the Chinese company. For its intended purpose, "the RTR weld was as good as you get," Cox declared unequivocally. Panzella rolled her eyes and shook her head in response to this description.

"Judge, I really have an issue with Ms. Panzella shaking her head like that in the presence of the jury," said Fuerth, rising to his feet.

"Ms. Panzella, please refrain from such displays," Mendez warned her.

"I'm Italian!" she replied coyly. "I can't help expressing myself."

Fuerth groaned.

March 31

"Congratulations to the Record Holders for the Most Dedicated, Diligent, Awe-Inspiring Jurors EVER! Thank you," read the inscription.

When we returned to the jury room yesterday, a surprise awaited us: a sheet cake with the above salutation, a reward from one of Room 452's jury clerks—*not* the woman with whom Alison had butted heads. Apparently, our service just made history as the longest ever in New York County (aka the borough of Manhattan).

Today's *New York Post* included an article, titled *Sweet Justice,* about our edible award. In flagrant violation of the judge's rule against reading newspaper articles about the case, we each pored over its contents, reveling in our fifteen minutes of fame.

"If you ever need your fellow citizens' help, you should hope for a jury like this," senior clerk Shawny Carroll told the newspaper. "They want to make sure it's done right. They're here four days a week. They've had to change their whole lives. Something like that needs to be appreciated." At the end of the piece, a killjoy defense attorney called our feat a "dubious distinction." Deep down, I knew he was right.

April 28

Like the jury, Cox also broke a record in this trial: He finally ended his testimony today, after eleven days on the stand, longer than any other witness (so far).

As part of his effort to prove that the Chinese weld's defects were harmless, and did not cause the accident, Cox handed us a smorgasbord of actual samples. As I held them in my hands, I was transported back to the "Introduction to Geology" course I'd taken in college. I never could recognize the difference between "igneous" and "metamorphic" (as in rock) back then, and I certainly didn't see the difference between "*inter*granular" and "*intra*granular" (as in crack) right now.

As he droned on, Cox did not even attempt to explain his esoteric subject to us jurors. He did, however, occasionally attempt to lighten his scientific verbiage with a little humor. For example, at one point in his testimony, Cox used the word "winch." Fuerth, brow furrowed, interrupted him.

"Do you mean *wench?*" he asked. Earlier in the trial, Fuerth had joked that he's no "Bob the Builder," but I'd have thought a lawyer who's dedicated his career to construction litigation would know what a winch is. Maybe, I thought, Fuerth was exaggerating his ignorance to cozy up to the jury.

"No, I mean *winch,*" replied Cox. "It's a lifting device. A wire rope *winch*, not a bar *wench.*" Cox grinned. "There *is* a difference."

Cox may have thought his reference to a floozy was funny, but he'd seriously misread our jury, who sat in unsmiling disgust.

What caused this supposedly "good-as-you-get" weld to break? Not a gradual accumulation of cracks, due to the normal movements of the crane. "This weld could have easily withstood that kind of stress," Cox insisted. "Rather, the weld broke due to a sudden, extreme event. This happened in a fraction of a second, like a lightning bolt."

I was expecting Cox to announce that the singular event that broke the weld was Don Leo's mishandling of the crane. He never did. So, inexplicably, we jurors were left to infer that this was Cox's conclusion. I added this to the gradual accumulation of head-scratchers in my notebook.

I guess Fuerth will put a second expert on the stand to prove that Don operated the crane in error. He'll have to. This, after all, is the very foundation of his defense.

April 30

Fuerth's last witness regarding the issue of liability was *not* the one I was expecting.

He *didn't* call an expert to testify that Don Leo had misused the crane, causing a perfectly adequate weld to snap, and leading to the deadly accident.

In fact, it seemed that Fuerth had given up on his operator-error theory altogether. Instead, he waved the white flag, in an effort to minimize rather than prevent casualties on his side of the aisle.

Fuerth tried to persuade the jury to find liable only New York Crane, and not Mr. Lomma himself, or the other company named in this lawsuit, J.F. Lomma. (There are actually two J.F. Lomma entities, Fuerth reminded us, both of which are on trial here: one incorporated in New Jersey, and the other in Delaware.) Such a finding would be good for Fuerth's client because it would limit any damages the plaintiffs are awarded to whatever New York Crane could pay on its own, leaving the resources of J. F. Lomma, and Mr. Lomma's personal assets, untouched.

To convince us to pin all the blame on just New York Crane, Fuerth put the comptroller for Lomma's businesses, Phil Mascolo, on the stand.

Mascolo claimed that Lomma's companies are completely independent from one another, apart from some minor logistical overlap, such as shared back-office personnel and payroll accounts. (A lightbulb went off in my head: Those seemingly irrelevant questions Fuerth had posed in his cross-examination of Lomma way back in December last year—the ones about his companies' organizational setup—were intended to bolster this claim. Now I knew where that puzzle piece fits!) "New York Crane alone owned the Kodiak crane that collapsed, so New York Crane alone is responsible for it," insisted Mascolo.

The plaintiffs, by contrast, argued that *all* the Lomma entities are liable, because New York Crane, J.F. Lomma, and Mr. Lomma himself are inextricably linked. Why do the plaintiffs want the jury to believe that they are all liable? So the money pot will be as big as possible.

Mascolo's first trap was set by O'Neill, who suggested that Lomma's cranes, including the Kodiak at issue in this case, are actually passed around from one Lomma company to another.

"Does J.F. Lomma of Delaware own any cranes?" O'Neill began.

"No," responded Mascolo.

"Let me show you this agreement between J.F. Lomma of Delaware and a company called Stevenson Crane," O'Neill continued. "What kind of contract is this?"

"It looks like a lease agreement with an option to buy," said Mascolo, shifting in his seat.

"If J.F. Lomma of Delaware doesn't own any cranes, how can it sell one?"

"I don't know."

Williams asked for a brief sidebar before trap number two, bringing Lomma personally into the mix, was set, this time by Slattery, the concrete subcontractor's attorney.

"Mr. Mascolo, here's a property tax bill for the J.F. Lomma, Inc., office in New Jersey," said Slattery. "Who is named as the owner?"

"Mr. Lomma," replied Mascolo.

"Who paid the bill?"

"J.F. Lomma, Inc."

When O'Neill began setting a third trap, Williams asked to approach the bench again.

"Oh, my God," huffed Panzella.

"Judge, there's no need for 'Oh, my God' from Ms. Panzella," said Fuerth, defending his associate.

"But we were just up here!" Panzella exclaimed.

"Enough with the speeches," added her son.

"Speeches?!" interjected Fuerth.

"Yeah. I'm tired of hearing them," Panzella's son complained.

"All of you, get up here *now*," intoned Mendez.

The lawyers huddled, heads bowed, while the judge scolded them.

When the sidebar ended, O'Neill continued his re-cross-examination of Mascolo.

"In June 2007, New York Crane owed J.F. Lomma, Inc., of New Jersey eleven and a half million dollars, correct?"

"Correct."

"You maintain, sir, that these companies operate independently?"

"Definitely."

"Sure," added O'Neill, flashing his Cheshire cat grin. "New York Crane owes J.F. Lomma eleven and a half million, and it operates independently."

"It's just an accounting entry."

"You told us you're not really the comptroller, that you're just an accountant, right?" O'Neill continued.

"I said, if people wish to call me the comptroller, it's fine with me," replied Mascolo meekly.

"So, who's really the comptroller? Is it Jimmy Lomma?"

"Jimmy Lomma's the president."

"*And* the comptroller?"

"No."

"There is no comptroller?"

"I am."

"You are. Now you're the comptroller again."

"If you wish to call me that, it's fine."

* * *

"I think all these Lomma entities are just paper companies," Martha said when we gathered in the jury room. "They're basically one and the same."

"I agree," I replied.

"O'Neill really humiliated that witness," Tony added.

I've got the perfect nickname for him, I thought: Mascolo the Emasculated.

May 1

Melanie handed each of us jurors the following letter this morning:

> Dear Jurors,
>
> If anyone feels they have not been treated appropriately during this trial by me, here is the phone number of my supervising judge, Peter Moulton, whom you are free to call.
>
> Sincerely, Hon. Manuel J. Mendez

I had two reactions.

One: I've met Peter Moulton. He's one of my husband's law school friends. There must be thousands of J.D.s in this city. How come the ones Bob knows keep popping up in this trial? I'm going to have to show him this letter. Will this be the straw that breaks the camel's back, the connection that gets me kicked off the jury?

Two: What on earth did the judge mean by "inappropriate treatment"?

"Does anybody know what Mendez is talking about?" I asked the other jurors.

Martha looked at me like I'd fallen off the turnip truck. "Um, maybe he's referring to the fact that we're in the eighth month of the trial, and there's still no end in sight."

"Okay, but why are we getting this letter *now?*"

Erin piped up. "I think I know. I need more time to study for my exam to become a licensed engineer, and I've written Mendez several notes asking to be let go. He hasn't replied to any of them. So yesterday, I threatened to contact his boss."

Alison added, "He's ignored my messages, too. I've been offered a promotion, so I need to get back to work full-time."

I see what's going on here, I thought: Alison and Erin are in an unwitting competition to be let go first, because Mendez could risk a mistrial if he dismisses them both. He needs a cushion, in case, God forbid, one of us gets sick or has some other type of emergency.

Erin's threat worked: She was released from jury duty at the end of the day.

There are eight remaining jurors, and I'm now a regular.

Hallelujah! I'll definitely get to take part in deliberations. (I showed Mendez's letter to Bob when I got home, and he didn't think his connection to Peter Moulton was a problem.)

May 4

At the end of the day, the judge told us we'd have yet another break, this one two weeks long. "Juror Number Five has a long-planned anniversary trip with her husband," Mendez explained.

Back in the jury room, Martha said sheepishly, "Sorry to put the trial on hold."

Deep down, I was annoyed by this delay, but I held my tongue. That's because I've got my own dirty secret: I have a vacation planned for next month that I haven't told anyone about yet.

June 1

This morning, Mendez called us, one by one, into his chambers. *Now* what's wrong? I wondered as Melanie ushered me in.

"Did you hear about yesterday's accident on Madison Avenue?" the judge asked. (A crane had dropped a giant rooftop air conditioning unit, injuring at least ten people.)

"Yes, sir. I saw something about it on the news before I had a chance to turn the TV off," I replied.

"Ms. Karten commented on the accident," Mendez continued. "Did you see that interview?"

"No, sir," I replied truthfully.

"Good. Will knowing about the accident affect how you view *this* case?"

"No, sir," I answered, again honestly.

"Okay. Thank you. You may go. Please ask the next juror to enter."

In truth, none of us had seen Karten's interview, and Mendez allowed the trial to continue.

* * *

Now that there are only seven jurors left (Mendez finally let Alison go), rumor has it that Lomma's team has a last-ditch strategy: Drag the proceeding out until we lose two more jurors, and Mendez will be forced to declare a mistrial.

Why would this be a good outcome for Lomma? Because the plaintiffs' lawyers, exhausted of energy and resources, would more than likely refrain from starting anew. Instead, they'd settle out of court, for a lot less money than they might have obtained through a trial.

I believed the rumor. During the last two weeks of May, Fuerth put on a string of witnesses who seemed so inconsequential that I didn't bother to write about them in my diary. (One was an insurance adjuster who seemed to be in Lomma's pocket, yet still managed to do Fuerth's client more harm than good.) I believed their sole purpose was, indeed, to eat up time.

In any case, I don't think counselor Fuerth's new game plan will work. Yesterday, I got an email from a long-ago colleague alerting me to a job opportunity. I wasn't interested. After all this effort, I'm not about to quit the trial, and I think my remaining colleagues feel the same way.

* * *

At the end of the day, we met ex-jurors Guy, Kayla, Erin, and Alison at a nearby bar. (We didn't invite Mary, because nobody knew how to get in touch with her.) They updated us on their lives "on the outside."

"I love my new job," Alison beamed.

Guy's new "project" is hush-hush, but he told us it was going well.

"How was your exam?" I asked Erin.

"I passed," she replied demurely.

"Congrats, Erin," said Kayla. "Let's order pickle backs!"

I had no idea what a pickle back was. The waitress brought a tray loaded with shot glasses, and Kayla demonstrated: She downed first a shot of whiskey, then a shot of pickle juice. I tried to follow suit, but I'm such a lightweight that it took me three sips to finish just the whiskey portion of the drink.

While we still-jurors updated the "retirees" on the trial, a group even larger than ours barreled into the bar, bedecked in softball attire. I correctly assumed it was one of those company leagues, and when they walked by our table, I noticed the letters "Arup" inscribed on their jerseys. I nudged Martha and whispered: "Arup's the engineering firm that investigated the accident for the plaintiffs!"

"You're right," she replied. "One of their employees

[about whom I did not write in my diary] testified at the beginning of the trial."

"I'm gonna say hello." I picked the friendliest looking member of the team, and explained who I was.

"I didn't work on the Ninety-First Street matter, but I've heard a lot about it," replied the young woman I'd chosen. "I can't believe the trial isn't over yet!"

I resisted the temptation to tell her more about the case, since such communication is verboten, and resorted to small talk.

When I left the bar, I walked past the back of the criminal courthouse. A gate was being raised to allow a police-escorted van to exit. Are there prisoners inside, I wondered with a shudder? Lomma escaped *that* fate, I thought, but we'll give him his just deserts.

June 2

"I feel like the last one remaining in the 'Ten Little Indians' poem," declared Fuerth self-pityingly in the courtroom this morning.

The lawyers for the general contractor, the codevelopers, and the condominium have all disappeared. Even though Fuerth was *not* the only one left at the defendants' table—his associate, Williams, remained, as did Slattery and Fumo—it seemed that Fuerth's client, rather than Slattery's or Fumo's, was now the plaintiffs' sole target.

I was confused by this new scenario. Since the start of the trial, I'd been under the impression that the Leo and

Kurtaj estates were suing *all* the defendants, end of story. When a defendant quit the proceeding, I assumed it was because the plaintiffs had settled with this party. If Sorbara and Brady Marine are still here, I reasoned, it must be because the plaintiffs are still after them.

But lately the plaintiffs' lawyers have ignored Brady Marine and have continued to stick up for Sorbara, so I wasn't so sure.

I've been tempted to ask the other jurors if they get what's going on, but I decided that would be *way* over the "no discussing the case" line.

* * *

This afternoon, Slattery, for defendant Sorbara, and Fumo, for defendant Brady Marine, had their turns addressing the issue of liability. Both put on experts who testified competently that the Chinese weld, and thus Lomma (and/or his companies), were to blame for the accident. In my opinion, they needn't have bothered. The jury had that figured out a *long* time ago.

* * *

At the end of the day, Judge Mendez announced another break from the case, this time because of yours truly (with a few additional days tacked on because Fumo, Brady Marine's attorney, was getting married). I hoped my fellow jurors didn't hate me. Aisha might, but not because of the delay I've caused. "I wish I could afford a vacation," she sighed as we said goodbye in the jury room.

SIX

THE DEFENDANTS' CASE: DAMAGES

June 22

Having finished putting on his (weak) case regarding liability, Fuerth turned today to the issue of damages. Naturally, he wants to keep both types—economic and noneconomic—as low as possible.

Unlike the plaintiffs, who had addressed economic damages first, Fuerth made noneconomic damages (for pre-impact fear, plus post-impact pain and suffering) his first order of business.

Fuerth began with Don Leo. Fuerth's primary objective was to convince us jurors that it took the crane's cab—with Don inside—mere seconds to fall, thereby keeping the amount of time Don suffered to a minimum. Fuerth would also suggest that the amount of time Don was conscious, and thus able to experience fear and pain, was even shorter.

To accomplish these goals, Fuerth called to the stand Dr. Ronald Fijalkowski, an expert in biomedical engineering, a field that analyzes the mechanics of human injury.

Before Fuerth had a chance to ask Fijalkowski a single question, Panzella tried to prevent this witness from testifying.

"*Voir dire,* your Honor?" Panzella asked the judge.

"Go ahead," he sighed in reply.

"Mr. Fijalkowski, you're not a biologist, are you?" Panzella huffed.

"No, ma'm," he replied.

"You're not a licensed engineer."

"No, ma'm."

"You're not a medical doctor."

"No, ma'm."

"Your Honor," Panzella turned toward Judge Mendez. "I don't think this man is qualified to do *anything.*"

Fuerth asked, "May I go on with this witness's testimony, judge?"

Mendez nodded affirmatively.

Disgusted by Mendez's decision, Panzella slammed her leaning tower of hot-pink and baby-blue folders down in front of her as she retook her seat.

Fijalkowski had an air of polished inoffensiveness, likely honed during the one hundred litigation matters—mostly car crashes, and seventy-five percent of them for defendants—he works on each year. A thirty-something-year-old, he focused his piercing blue eyes on the jury and smiled in a comradely manner when he delivered each polite response.

As for the length of time it took the crane to fall, Fijalkowski estimated that the entire collapse lasted no more than twenty-five seconds.

This was such a miniscule amount of time that it seemed to me we could stop right there: Fuerth's expert thinks Don experienced about half a minute of terror, plus pain and suffering. But Fijalkowski was asked to dissect his estimate to the enth degree. "It would have taken Mr. Leo two to three seconds to react to the popping sound that signaled the beginning of the collapse," he added, "which reduces the period for potential damages to twenty-two or twenty-three seconds."

Come on! I thought. Is each second really that important?

Fijalkowski went on to claim that Don would not have sustained any physical injuries—and therefore would not have experienced any pain and suffering—before the crane hit the building across Ninety-First Street, debunking Schwartz's theory that Don's arms and legs had broken *before* this collision. "I believe those injuries, plus his skull fracture—which would have rendered Mr. Leo unconscious—occurred either when the crane hit this building, or when it hit the ground."

Panzella was not about to let Fijalkowski, whose opinion was a serious threat to her client's potential award (and the one-third of it that constitutes her fee), leave the stand without putting him through the wringer. She berated this "pawn of the insurance industry" for not doing his homework: He *didn't* read so-and-so's testimony; he *didn't* contact the City's building department; and he *didn't* go to the accident site.

This was one of Panzella's favorite, and to my mind, least effective tactics: ridiculing her adversaries' witnesses for not performing tasks they had no need to carry out. She might just as well have asked Fijalkowski why he himself had never jumped off the Empire State Building to find out what sort of injuries he would suffer.

Panzella even insisted that, as a robust former athlete (Don had played football in high school), Don's reaction time to the sound of the weld breaking would have been instantaneous. "So, Mr. Fijalkowski, Don would have suffered two or three seconds longer than you claimed, right?" Panzella asked tartly. If Panzella cares this much about a few seconds, I guess each one is, indeed, worth a lot of money. Before participating in this case, I never would have believed that damage awards could be this finely calibrated.

* * *

During a break, I chatted with Martha, the retired therapist on our jury. "You know, this trial is personal for me," she confided. "My father started out as an air-conditioning mechanic. In his line of work, a crane could easily have fallen on top of him and killed him."

Here was a pro-plaintiff bias of which the defense is totally unaware, I thought.

June 24

Today Fuerth called a second witness regarding the non-economic damages owed to Don Leo, perhaps in an effort to make up for the lack of witnesses he'd put on the stand regarding liability.

Dr. Mark Taff, a forensic pathologist, began with a dramatic declaration: "There are five categories of death: instantaneous; near instantaneous; rapid; slow; and chronic."

According to Taff, Don's death fits in the second category, "near instantaneous." Taff agreed with Fijalkowski that Don experienced a maximum of twenty-five seconds of distress.

Even though the law distinguishes pre-impact terror from post-impact pain and suffering, Taff told us the two cannot be separated. "You can't sever the mind from the body," Taff claimed. (So, according to Taff, I *hadn't* been off base when I questioned the legitimacy of this division during Schwartz's testimony for the plaintiffs.) "In fact, if you fear for your life, this feeling actually *increases* your pain and suffering."

Despite the gift this witness gave her—the claim that Don's fear *increased* his pain, making it more "valuable"— Panzella attacked Taff's competence in much the same way she had attacked Fijalkowski's.

"Panzella's never satisfied," I whispered to one of the jurors.

"I know. It's annoying, but it does make her a good advocate," she muttered in reply.

In the afternoon, Taff turned his attention to Ramadan Kurtaj (about whom Fijalkowski had not testified). He placed Ramadan in the "rapid" death category, claiming that his fear, along with pain and suffering, lasted a total of about thirty minutes. "Initially, Mr. Kurtaj experienced a ten on the pain scale," Taff allowed. "But once his multiple injuries reduced his blood flow, there was decreased oxygen, and he entered what's called a hypoxic state. This is a condition in which the brain cannot perceive the sensations typically relayed from the outside world to the central nervous system."

In other words, as time went on, Ramadan felt less fear and pain.

In cross-examination, Karten asked Taff about the notation in Ramadan's hospital records that suggested he had regained some level of consciousness just before eleven o'clock in the morning. "If this documentation is correct," Taff replied, "I would increase the length of time that Mr. Kurtaj experienced pain and suffering to a total of two hours and fifty minutes." With this statement, Taff did Karten a remarkable favor, just as he had Panzella. He could have dismissed the notation outright as a mistake, or claimed that Ramadan regained consciousness only temporarily.

"Why didn't Fuerth keep Taff from making these concessions?" I wrote in my notebook.

* * *

All this talk about death got me thinking about one my favorite poets, Emily Dickinson. When I got home, I leafed through a collection of her work.

As I read "Suspense—is Hostiler than Death," it struck me that, in the context of this trial, Dickinson could be talking about pre-impact terror. I wondered: Would this poet have been able to assign a monetary value to the morbid sensations she described?

June 25

This morning, Aisha brought a homemade flan to the jury room for us to sample.

"This is delicious," I told her.

"Thanks," she replied. "I'm gonna start my own business, called "My Sweet Tooth," selling baked goods over the internet. Sandra and some of the other jurors are helping me set it up."

Sandra's well-situated to advise Aisha, because she has her own online business, selling fashion accessories inspired by the designs of artisans in her native Colombia. Sandra pulled me aside. "Serving as a juror, and giving Aisha advice, it's kind of new to me," she confided. "Helping people—beyond my family and friends—is a nice feeling." I guess jury duty's getting Sandra out of her bubble, too.

Then I wondered if Sandra might actually be biased

toward Lomma, since he's a fellow entrepreneur. No way: Lomma's too big-time to instill empathy in Sandra. She'll go with the little guys, Don and Ramadan.

As will I. At the beginning of the case, I'd vowed not to succumb to the appeal of the Davids (that is, the plaintiffs) in the story behind this trial. But at this point, I've given up. Since my bias seems to jibe with most of the evidence presented over the past nine months, I've decided it's more than okay to stop fighting it.

June 29

Having completed his case regarding damages for pre-impact fear, plus pain and suffering, today Fuerth called a witness to address economic damages.

Because Panzella had, mysteriously, not elicited any testimony regarding Don's earnings, Fuerth needed to tackle Ramadan's income only. Unsurprisingly, Fuerth's expert opined that Ramadan would have made much less money than Karten's expert did. This witness suggested that we award Ramadan's parents a mere two hundred thousand dollars, and Selvi a maximum of three million, in economic damages.

* * *

As we packed up in the jury room at the end of the day, Aisha showed me a video on her phone of her youngest son, who is autistic. He was flailing on the ground as Aisha tried to get him on the waiting school bus. "He's getting so big, it's harder and harder for me to control him lately," Aisha sighed.

Somehow, just about everyone in this courthouse, including the jurors, the lawyers, and the judge on this case, plus the clerks in the jury assembly room and other staffers, knows about Aisha's son. On World Autism Day, we had all worn blue, the disorder's trademark color, to support her. Aisha appreciated the gesture.

I think the trial may provide Aisha with a welcome distraction from the difficulties of her home life, just as it provides me with a welcome distraction from the tedium of mine.

And we may not be the only jurors benefitting from the change of pace courthouse life affords: The cops, Tony and Aaron, are getting to "work" regular, comparatively stress-free hours; and Sandra is getting to "work" alongside people, instead of being cooped up alone in her home-based business.

July 14

Today we heard the rest of a deposition for defendant Lomma, the first part of which had been read to us several weeks ago. Not only was I unable to remember what that first part had been about, but I had no idea what this second part was about, either. As I listened in bafflement, I surprised myself by raising my hand. "What on earth *is* this?" I shouted.

The judge, taken aback, apologized rather than reprimanding me for my outburst, then repeated the names of the man who had been deposed and the company where he works. But this didn't help at all: What I needed was context, someone to explain, "This is important for X, Y, and Z reasons." Someone to tell me where this puzzle piece fits. As was all-too-often the case in this trial, I didn't understand the "why" behind this evidence. Resigned, I slumped in my seat and stared at the ceiling.

When the reading was over, testimony for defendant Lomma came to an unceremonious end.

* * *

Curiously, the attorneys for defendants Sorbara and Brady Marine called not a single witness regarding damages, either economic or noneconomic. Perhaps, I thought, they'd decided that Fuerth had done such a good job that they could rely on his witnesses alone to keep damages to a minimum, no matter who ends up paying them.

Or maybe Slattery and Fumo were so confident that their clients would *not* be found liable that they'd decided to save a few bucks by forgoing the costly services of expert witnesses.

Or maybe the judge, having used up most of his patience, told Slattery and Fumo, "Look, we don't need to hear anything further from you guys. Done and done!"

* * *

On my way home, I remembered that today is Bastille Day, a turning point in the French Revolution, whose participants had been mollified with cake from a queen. Today was also a turning point in the trial, whose jurors had been mollified with cake from a jury clerk.

Now it was time for the lawyers' summations. I prayed that they would wrap up their cases more quickly than they had unwrapped them at the beginning, way back in October last year.

SEVEN

CLOSING STATEMENTS
AND
JURY INSTRUCTIONS

July 16

At long last, it was time for the lawyers to conclude their stories.

Fumo, for defendant Brady Marine, went first. As he began his closing statement, Fumo looked even paler than usual—almost the color of the whiteboard on which he laid out his principal arguments. He mistakenly wrote "point number four" instead of "three," then attempted to erase his error in frustration, having inadvertently used a permanent marker. The jurors evinced looks of pity before Fumo was rescued by Panzella, who handed him an erasable pen from her ever-impressive stash of stationary supplies.

During his summation, Fumo referred periodically to the verdict sheets, which will allow the jury to apportion a percentage of liability to each of the remaining defendants, as well as to Don Leo. Up to this point, we jurors hadn't even known for sure that we'd be able to divide up liability in this manner. (I thought we might be required to put *all* the blame on *one* party only.)

"One of your easiest decisions," contended Fumo, "will be whether or not Brady Marine caused this accident." Obviously, Fumo continued, his client, who was not asked to test the Chinese weld, whose welding did not negatively affect this weld, and whose own weld remained intact after the accident, is zero percent at fault.

Next up was Slattery, for defendant Sorbara. "I'm really gonna miss you guys," he said, looking right at the jury. "I've been living with you for eleven months. Some marriages," he chuckled, "are shorter than that."

Unlike Fumo, who hadn't even mentioned Lomma or his companies in his wrap-up, Slattery reviewed both the blamelessness of his client, Sorbara, and the fault of Fuerth's clients. By the end of the day, Slattery wasn't even close to finishing his so-called "summary."

Why has Slattery suddenly taken a leaf out of Panzella's playbook by being so long-winded? I wondered.

July 20

"You jurors can finally see the light at the end of the tunnel, *and it's not the headlights of an oncoming train* [my italics]," began Fuerth's closing statement.

Naturally the jury doesn't see the end of the trial as a threat, I thought. Quite the opposite. Was Fuerth projecting onto us his own fear—that he'll be hit by a freight car of fury when we find one or more of his clients liable?

(That's right, I wrote *when:* I think Fuerth knows he's going to lose.)

Lomma's lawyer went on to display the many chips on his shoulder. The plaintiffs and the other defendants ganged up on him: "I'm standing before you with the sniper scope's red dot between my eyes." His client was far from perfect: "Lomma's no Brad Pitt," and "he doesn't speak the Queen's English." He couldn't fully explain his operator-error theory of the collapse: "The judge ruled I couldn't call certain witnesses to support my argument, and I just have to live with that."

Did Fuerth think that we jurors would go easier on Lomma and his companies if we felt sorry for *him?* If so, it didn't work on me.

Fuerth then went on to rehash all the reasons why Lomma and his companies weren't liable for the accident.

That was a waste of time, I thought.

If you knew we weren't going to believe you, how was this an effective strategy? I wished I could ask Fuerth. To my mind, it would have been better for him to gamble on the following approach: "Okay, I admit it: My client made a mistake. Mr. Lomma feels awful about what happened. It was never his intention for anyone to be hurt or killed. Please don't be too hard on him. He'll be much more careful from now on."

Remember when I wondered if our jury's religious beliefs would affect our decisions in this trial? If Fuerth's client had appeared the least bit repentant, we might have been persuaded to punish him less harshly. Perhaps,

I thought, Fuerth had proposed this admittedly risky approach, but the imperious Lomma, too proud to admit any wrongdoing, had nixed it.

In any case, after his ineffective defense, Fuerth went on to address the issue of damages.

He suggested we award three hundred thousand dollars for the total of Don Leo's pre-impact terror and post-impact pain and suffering; for his mother's lost economic support, Fuerth proposed zero, discounting entirely Maria's testimony that Don had helped her out financially.

For the total of Ramadan Kurtaj's pre-impact terror and post-impact pain and suffering, Fuerth proposed two and a half million dollars. Based on his forensic accountant's analysis, Fuerth suggested a quarter million in lost financial support for Ramadan's parents, and a maximum of three million for his widow.

I had no idea how Fuerth determined the amounts he proposed for noneconomic damages for either plaintiff. I hoped they were based on some standard—maybe the amounts awarded in previous cases for similar types of suffering—and not on a whim. I assumed Judge Mendez would enlighten us on this issue before we deliberate.

I did some quick math: If we jurors were to follow Fuerth's suggestions to the letter, his clients would be out to the tune of about six million dollars. Didn't seem like enough. I glanced at the other jurors to gauge their response to Fuerth's proposals, but they remained steely-eyed.

At this juncture, I was expecting the judge to announce a break. Instead, Fuerth sprung a surprise: The jury would have to decide whether the plaintiffs deserved so-called "punitive damages," he told us. The purpose of this type of award, he explained, is to punish the defendant for reckless misconduct, and to deter him and others from similar misbehavior in the future. To deliver such an award, we would have to find that Lomma *knowingly* leased equipment that might cause injury or death. Fuerth claimed Lomma believed the crane was safe, so punitive damages are not warranted.

* * *

And this was not the only unexpected responsibility Fuerth rested at our feet: "You will have to decide whether to 'pierce the corporate veil' of Mr. Lomma individually and his companies," Fuerth told us.

Do what now? Not once has the expression "pierce the corporate veil" been uttered in this trial, and I had no idea what it meant.

Happily, Fuerth defined our second new task immediately. "To pierce the corporate veil, the jury must find that the assets of Mr. Lomma personally and his companies are intermingled, and that the corporations overlap in other ways as well."

Fuerth told us we should not pierce the corporate veil, that if we do find fault on the part of any of his clients, as he had previously stated, it should be New York Crane and New York Crane alone.

In the musical *Rent,* a year is measured in "seasons of love" or "cups of coffee."

In this nearly year-long proceeding, it's measured in "days of testimony," of which there have been one hundred and thirteen so far, or "pages of transcript," of which there are twenty-one thousand and counting.

These were the impressively horrifying statistics Karten presented at the beginning of her closing statement in New York County's longest-ever trial.

Swathed in a crisp white dress whose bell sleeves were the same shape as a nun's wimple—a savvy saleswoman, Karten's apparel choices were loaded with symbolism—she reached for the heavens, claiming that "Don and Ramadan's spirits will be joined together forever because of the way they died, and because of this case."

Karten addressed the two new issues that Fuerth had told us we would have to decide. Regarding punitive damages, she claimed that Lomma had, indeed, known that his crane was deadly. "The actions of Lomma and his companies were wanton and reckless and showed a complete disregard for human life, safety, and the public at large," she declared unequivocally. By awarding punitive damages, Karten told us, "you jurors can do what the judge in the criminal trial failed to do: punish Lomma for a criminal act." We can be the heroes in Karten's story.

As for piercing the corporate veil, Karten stated, "Our position is that these companies are a joint enterprise.

James Lomma is the president of all of them. He owns all the stock. In order for us to make sure we have all the right parties, that we get complete accountability, the corporate veil *must* be pierced."

Before Karten made her suggestions regarding the amount of our awards, she pointed to another hero in her story, Ramadan himself. "He fought in one of the worst wars in the world, the war for Kosovo's independence. Ramadan made it out only to be killed by a crane here in America." After seven years, added Karten, "the Kurtaj family deserves closure."

Karten started with economic damages. For lost financial support for Ramadan's parents, she recommended just over two million dollars; for his widow, she suggested about five and a quarter million (magnanimously acknowledging that O'Neill's client deserved more in economic damages than did her own).

For Ramadan's pre-impact terror: ten million. For his pain and suffering: twenty-five million.

I was flabbergasted by the enormity of the last two numbers.

Karten went on to suggest the manner in which we should break down liability, among Lomma and his companies only, and not Sorbara, Brady Marine, or Don Leo.

I paid no attention. I was still reeling from the thirty-five million dollars Karten had proposed for the total of Ramadan's pre- and post-impact distress.

* * *

Packing up at the end of the day, I wondered if the other jurors had been as stunned by Karten's suggestions as I had. Everyone kept mum: Now that we were so close to deliberations, when we would finally be allowed to discuss the case to our hearts' content, it was a lot easier to follow the rule to keep our thoughts to ourselves.

July 23

It was standing room only in the courtroom today. Members of Don Leo's union, clad in hardhats and work boots, filled the benches and leaned against the walls to support Panzella during her closing argument. She proudly pointed out their presence to the jury, and noted, in disgust, the absence of Mr. Lomma.

Referencing Lomma's original sin, the removal of the evidentiary crack in the fallen crane's first bearing, Panzella quoted no less than Mahatma Gandhi: "The moment there is suspicion about a person's motives, everything he does becomes tainted." All of Lomma's subsequent misdeeds, according to Panzella, added up to full blame for him and his companies.

As for our damage awards, Panzella threw up her hands, claiming she couldn't distinguish Don's pre-impact terror from his post-impact pain and suffering. "I will leave that to you," she told the jury. "It's beyond my experience to know how you should divide those two things."

Huh? If a personal injury attorney doesn't know how to do this, how does she expect us regular folks to know how?

In any case, based on the fact that the accident began at a few minutes before eight o'clock in the morning, and that the death certificate states the time of death as 8:22 a.m., Panzella claimed Don was alive and conscious for up to twenty-seven minutes after the collapse began.

For the total of Don's distress, Panzella suggested we award thirty to forty million dollars, in essence the same total Karten had proposed for Ramadan (even though Don's suffering didn't last nearly as long as Ramadan's did). In addition, Panzella proposed we give Maria Leo one and a half million to two and three quarter million for lost in-kind support—that is, all the chores Don did for her.

We should award punitive damages, said Panzella, "because Mr. Lomma owns three hundred and eighty cranes, which is how many more accidents could happen if you don't stop him."

Panzella ended her summation with a sputter: "I wish I had a nice wrap thing to tell you, but I don't have it in me." Come on, lady! I thought. After all the work you've put into this trial, you couldn't muster the inner strength to deliver a proper ending to your story?

The day ground to a halt with the following statement from Judge Mendez: "What remains is for me to charge you on the law, and for you to deliberate. But I don't want you to begin deliberations in a case of this magnitude on a Friday. So, we will not be working tomorrow. I will see you on Monday at nine-thirty."

The jury filed out in weary silence, stymied by yet another delay.

July 27

"Neither I nor anyone else may invade your province," Judge Mendez proclaimed this morning. The "province" in question, exclusively the jury's, is the factual realm. According to Mendez, we alone get to decide which facts are real, and which aren't.

I was expecting the rest of the "jury charge" (the judge's pre-deliberation instructions) to take several minutes at most, and I was champing at the bit. Instead, it took him a few hours to deliver his complicated directions. How silly of me to think an eleven-month trial would come with simple instructions.

How are we supposed to remember them all? I wondered. Before closing statements, our journals had been taken away from us, so we couldn't take notes. (We'll get them back when we deliberate.) I hoped that, between the six of us, we'd be able to recall the most important ones.

Mendez reminded us that we must accept the law as he gives it to us, even if we don't agree with it. In actuality, juries *can* disregard a law they find unjust—known as "jury nullification"—but the judge naturally didn't want to encourage such insurgent behavior.

"As a matter of law," Mendez continued, "the jury may not hold liable the City of New York." This was a maddening, never explained prohibition. As I've said, it seemed obvious that the City, with its poor oversight and confusing regulations, was partly at fault. What's more, I know the City *can* be sued for causing an accident—case in point, all those pothole injury lawsuits advertised on TV by personal injury lawyers. (The judge didn't even mention RTR, the Chinese company that manufactured the allegedly defective bearing, and I still didn't understand why it wasn't being held liable either.)

His Honor's next instruction: There are two types of evidence for us to evaluate, direct and circumstantial. Mendez explained the difference using a simple yet flawed example.

"Let us suppose that a fact in dispute is whether I knocked over a glass of water near the witness chair. If someone testifies that he or she saw me knock over the glass, that is direct evidence.

"But what if a witness says he saw the glass on the bench," Mendez continued, "and while he was looking the other way, he heard the breaking of glass, looked up, and saw me wiping water from my clothes and from the papers on the bench? This is circumstantial evidence from which you could reasonably infer that I knocked over the glass.

"However, what if the water glass is equidistant from the court clerk and me," the judge added, "and when the witness looks up, he sees both of us brushing water from our clothes? You wouldn't be able to decide on the evidence alone who knocked over the glass. But if the witness also testified that he heard the clerk say, 'I'm sorry,' you could infer that it was the clerk."

The devil's advocate in me wanted to raise my hand and declare, "The clerk could be apologizing for splashing water on your clothes while drying off his own, and *not* for having knocked the glass over." But I held my tongue.

In any case, I was about to learn another something new about the law. Before this case, I'd been under the impression that circumstantial evidence was considered *less* reliable than direct evidence. But Judge Mendez told us that the former can be equally credible, or even more believable.

* * *

So how should we weigh the evidence? Consider the following, instructed the judge: "The interest or lack of interest of the witness in the outcome of the case. The bias or prejudice of the witness, if there be any. The age, the appearance, and the manner of the witness as he or she testified. The opportunity that the witness had to observe the facts about which he or she testified. The probability or improbability of the witness's testimony when considered in light of all the other evidence in the case."

Interestingly, the law allows us to disregard completely the entire testimony of a witness if we believe he made just one false statement about one material fact, which echoes the Gandhi quote Panzella referenced in her closing statement.

Mendez repeated the same advice he gave us at the beginning of the trial: "Use the tests you employ in your everyday affairs to judge each witness." That seemed easy at the outset, but from the vantage point of a seasoned juror, I see two problems with this guidance.

In real life, you can do as much of your own research as you like until you're able to make a sound evaluation. You aren't limited to the information others provide you, as you are in the courtroom.

Plus, the nature of the statements I hear in my "regular" life don't bear much resemblance to those I've heard in this trial. (Case in point: the statement by Ed Cox, Fuerth's scientific expert, that "we live in a world of imperfect welds.")

Mendez warned us that we may not share relevant life experiences, such as "professional expertise or other facts not in evidence," with our fellow jurors during deliberations. So, for example, if Erin had remained on the jury, she could have based some of her opinions on her knowledge as a structural engineer, but she wouldn't have been able to share them with us.

This was another prohibition that seemed ridiculous to me. Isn't a trial supposed to be a search for the whole truth, not some filtered half-truth?

As for the burden of proof, Mendez told us, it lies with the plaintiffs. They must establish liability by a "fair preponderance of the credible evidence." I didn't know what he meant by "fair" in this context, but I figured fifty-one percent or more would do it.

* * *

Next Mendez instructed us on piercing the corporate veil. To do so, the judge told us, we must find the following three elements: "The corporations are so intertwined that they are merely alter egos of one another; the corporations' owner completely controls the corporations; and the corporations' owner used this complete control to commit a fraud, or a dishonest or unjust act, in violation of the injured parties' rights."

Punitive damages are warranted, Mendez explained, for "conduct that represents a high degree of immorality and elicits the type of outrage frequently associated with a crime." The purpose of such damages is not to compensate the plaintiffs (although they *are* the sole recipients of the money), but to punish the defendants for acts that are "wanton and reckless"—the very adjectives Karten had used in her closing statement to describe Lomma's behavior.

The plaintiffs, Mendez added, must prove entitlement to punitive damages by "clear, unequivocal and convincing evidence. This means evidence that satisfies you that there is a high degree of probability that there was wanton and reckless conduct by the defendant." To award punitive damages, Mendez emphasized, "it is not enough to find that the preponderance of the evidence is in the plaintiffs' favor."

Finally, the judge addressed economic damages. He instructed us that Ramadan was "legally obligated" to support his wife, Selvi, whether or not we believe the marriage was a sham. He also reminded us that we cannot compensate the survivors for their own "sorrow, mental anguish, injury to feelings, or loss of companionship," another prohibition that, as I wrote earlier, I find unfair.

Mendez finished his instructions by addressing the nuts and bolts of deliberations. Our first order of business, he told us, would be to elect a foreperson, who is traditionally

Juror Number One. (This would be Sandra.) We must address the verdict sheets in chronological order—we may not skip a question that stumps us and come back to it later, like one can in a traditional test. We need not be unanimous: Five out of six of us must agree on each question before going on to the next one.

Then it hit me: We're not going to get any guidance from Mendez on determining the amounts we award in noneconomic damages. All we'll have to go on are Fuerth's and the plaintiffs' lawyers' suggestions, none of which appealed to me. How on earth were we mere mortals supposed to decide what a second, or a minute, or an hour of terror, plus pain and suffering, are worth?

Mendez finished with the following: "Remember, the dispute between the parties is, for them, a very important matter. They and the Court rely on you to give full and conscientious deliberation and consideration to the issues and evidence before you. By so doing, you carry out to the fullest your oath as jurors to truly try the issues of this case and to render a true verdict.

"The jury may now retire to deliberate."

EIGHT

DELIBERATIONS AND VERDICT

July 27 (continued)

When Judge Mendez told us it was time to start deliberating, we jurors got our mojo back. All of us, that is, except Shawn, who won't be allowed to participate because he's an alternate. The poor guy was still expected to come to court (in case one of us keels over), but he will be sequestered in a different room. I couldn't imagine his level of frustration at not being able to deliberate after all these months. I hoped he'd approve of our verdict. That was the least we could do for him.

* * *

The "final six" entered the jury room to find a make-your-own-sandwich spread, our first meal care of the lawyers. This was a "working lunch," so we tackled our first task, choosing a foreperson, while we tore into our free feast. "Martha and I were talking about it last night, and we nominate Aaron," said Aisha. I stole a glance at the de facto candidate, Sandra, to gauge her reaction. She replied nonchalantly, "Fine by me."

I probably would have suggested Martha (to honor her on-time diligence, plus the Smithie in me would have liked a woman to be in charge), but Aaron was a solid choice, and I wasn't going to rock the boat over this relatively pedestrian matter. Aaron won the position unanimously.

Our foreperson was about to read aloud the first question when I stopped him: "How about we say a prayer for Don and Ramadan?" I'm not particularly religious, but before we got knee-deep in the dollars and cents of the matter at hand, I felt the need to remind everyone—especially myself—that we were talking about the lives and deaths of two actual human beings.

I was afraid my colleagues would find my suggestion too kumbaya, but everyone agreed it was a good idea. We held hands and lowered our heads. Tony, possibly the most religious of the remaining jurors, said a few words. Then, with whatever "god" each of us had addressed watching over us, we got to work.

* * *

The set of questions for the estate of Donald Christopher Leo was seventeen pages long. Whoa! Once again, I guess I shouldn't have been surprised that a long trial would culminate in a long verdict.

The other time I'd been on a jury, we'd had one single question to answer: Is the defendant guilty or not guilty?

In that (criminal) proceeding, it took two days to agree on that one answer. This time, the jury got through its first question in a New York minute.

Question #1A: "Was James F. Lomma negligent?" That is, was he *personally* responsible for the accident?

"Yes," declared Tony.

"Absolutely," added Martha.

Everyone else nodded unhesitatingly in agreement.

Of course, no one had ever proved that Lomma *himself* had seen Wang's smoking-gun email, the one in which she said RTR had no confidence in its ability to perform the weld. But we didn't mention it. Either we'd forgotten this inconvenient truth, or, I'm ashamed to admit, we didn't care. We *had* to sic it on this baddest of bad guys.

Question #1B: "Was James F. Lomma's negligence a substantial factor in causing the crane accident?"

"Absent Lomma's negligence, the crane wouldn't have collapsed," I said. 'So, his negligence was necessarily a 'substantial factor' in causing the accident, right?"

"Right," everyone replied. Yeses all around.

Question #1C: "Were James F. Lomma's actions reckless and wanton?"

The answer to this question would determine whether we award punitive damages. "Does anybody remember exactly how Mendez defined those adjectives?" asked Aaron.

"I know what 'reckless' means, but I'd always thought a 'wonton' was a dumpling," someone quipped.

While we chuckled, Aaron wrote his first note, asking

for clarification. Then he knocked on the jury room door, which Melanie, who was stationed on a chair on the other side, opened immediately. She marched off to deliver the message to her boss.

A few minutes later, Judge Mendez himself entered the jury room. He reread the definition: "An act is wanton and reckless when it demonstrates conscious indifference to and utter disregard of its effects upon the health, safety, and rights of others."

I was so surprised that the judge had delivered the definition in person—I was expecting Melanie to hand it to us on a slip of paper—that I almost missed it. Nonetheless, I got the gist.

"Lomma didn't give a damn about the safety of others," said Aisha.

"All he cared about was money," added Sandra.

I joined the others in answering "Yes" to question #1C.

The eight subsequent questions were the same as the previous ones, except that they related to New York Crane and to J.F. Lomma, Inc.

"New York Crane owned the crane, so of course it was negligent and reckless," reasoned Aisha.

"And J.F. Lomma paid for the Chinese bearing, so it was complicit, too," added Martha.

We answered the group of questions regarding negligence on the part of New York Crane and J.F. Lomma in the affirmative.

Question #3A: "Did New York Crane and Equipment Corp. breach its warranty in that the Kodiak crane leased to

Sorbara Construction Corp. was not reasonably fit for its ordinary purpose?"

"Why are they even asking this question?" one of the jurors wondered. "If New York Crane was negligent, of course it breached its warranty."

"You're right," I replied.

We all agreed on "Yes" to this one, and the next, related question: *"Was New York Crane and Equipment Corp.'s breach of warranty a substantial factor in causing the crane accident?"*

* * *

I glanced at my watch. It was only two o'clock. I felt a tinge of guilt. "Does anyone think we're going too fast?" I asked.

"No," replied Aaron unequivocally. "We've been here so long, we all know what we think."

"Sitting through eleven months of evidence, we've already done the hard part," added Martha. "This part's easy."

Deep down I agreed, but I was still plagued by the feeling that we owed "a case of this magnitude," as Mendez had called it, a little more respect by slowing down.

Questions #5 and #6: "Should New York Crane's corporate veil be pierced so that Mr. Lomma individually, and J.F. Lomma, Inc., are liable for New York Crane's negligence?"

"If I learned one thing from the tedious testimony of Mascolo, Lomma's comptroller," said Tony, "it's that New York Crane shares *everything* with J.F. Lomma."

"And Lomma *personally* owns these companies lock, stock, and barrel," I added.

Yeses all around.

Question #7A: "Was Sorbara Construction Corp. negligent?", and Question #7B: "Was Sorbara Construction Corp.'s negligence a substantial factor in causing the accident?"

"Fuerth never proved that any Sorbara employee tampered with the safety switches," said Tony, "and he gave no reason for why they would even want to in the first place."

"And Fuerth never proved that Don [who was hired by Sorbara] did anything wrong on the morning of the accident," said Martha.

"He didn't have any hard evidence that *either* operator ever mishandled the crane," added Aaron.

"And I don't see how Sorbara could have known that there was something wrong with the weld," I said.

We all answered "no" to the first question, which meant we could skip the second one.

The next four questions were the same as the last two, except that they related to Brady Marine and Don Leo.

"Fuerth never proved that Brady's welding damaged the Chinese weld," Sandra said.

"Or that Lomma asked Brady to test it," added Aisha.

As for Don, even if the praise heaped on him by his fellow operator, John Samuels, was motivated by bias or self-interest, Fuerth never proved that Don did anything wrong. "No" answers all around.

We'd already reached Question #10, and so far, our deliberations had been short and sweet.

* * *

Question #10 finally got us talking: *"What is the percentage of fault for the following parties: a) James Lomma, individually; b) New York Crane; c) J.F. Lomma, Inc.; d) Sorbara; e) Brady Marine; and f) Don Leo?"*

"Of course, Sorbara, Brady, and Don are zero percent at fault," said Martha. "We already established that in our earlier answers."

"Yeah, why do we have to say it again?" asked Aisha.

"Because *everything* in this trial has to be repeated at least once," I joked.

We snickered, then returned to the remainder of our task: distributing fault among Lomma individually and his companies. In hopes that the jury would *not* pierce the corporate veil, Fuerth had urged us to put one hundred percent of the blame on New York Crane, the least wealthy Lomma entity. Karten, on the other hand, had proposed the following breakdown: seventy percent for Lomma personally; twenty percent for J.F. Lomma, Inc.; and ten percent for New York Crane.

"Why do we have to find one of these parties more or less liable than another?" I asked.

"Exactly," said Aisha. "I thought they were all in it together."

We shot looks of uncertainty at one another.

"Look, they've asked us to divvy up liability, so that's what we have to do," concluded Aaron. "I agree with Karten that Lomma should bear most of the responsibility."

Sandra, Tony, and I were on board with Aaron's opinion.

"But Varganyi's the one who ordered the bad bearing, and he worked for New York Crane," reasoned Aisha.

"Well, I think New York Crane's just a front," replied Martha," so I don't think it should be blamed at all."

"So, what do we do?" asked Sandra.

"Let's each write down our votes, and then we'll see if we can come to an agreement," suggested our sage foreman, Aaron.

This is how we voted:

	Cynthia	Sandra	Aaron	Martha	Tony	Aisha
James Lomma	65%	70%	60%	50%	60%	50%
J.F. Lomma, Inc.	20%	20%	20%	50%	30%	10%
New York Crane	15%	10%	20%	0%	10%	40%

After passing the results around, nobody seemed inclined to change his mind.

"I've got it," said Tony, grinning. "Let's calculate the average of our individual votes, and then vote on that average."

"Great idea," replied Aaron.

Someone, I don't remember who, pulled out a smartphone and used the calculator app to compute each average.

The result: sixty-one percent for Lomma, twenty percent for J.F. Lomma, Inc., and nineteen percent for New York Crane.

As I wrote this tonight, I rechecked these calculations several times, and came up with fifty-nine percent for Lomma, twenty-five percent for J.F. Lomma, Inc., and sixteen percent for New York Crane. Aargh. We got the math wrong. Did no one check it at the time? It wasn't a huge mistake—and at least the proportional breakdown was correct—but I felt contrite, nonetheless.

In any case, this question led to the only dissent in our verdict. "My own business is set up as a limited liability company," explained Sandra, "so that I can protect my personal assets. I know from experience that Lomma's trying to shield himself, and I don't want him to get away with it. I think he should pay more than sixty-one percent, so I'm going to vote no." (In voicing this opinion, Sandra broke the "no sharing of relevant life experiences" instruction, but I didn't blame her at all.)

Sandra wasn't so adamant that she tried to change our minds, and the vote went through, with the required five out of six agreeing to the compromise. But Sandra smiled broadly when she signed her name on the "dissenting juror" line of the verdict sheet.

* * *

The rest of the questions related to damages. The first was about our economic award: It asked us to state the value of Maria Leo's lost in-kind support. In her closing statement, Panzella had hesitatingly proposed between one and a half million and two and three quarter million dollars for this loss, based on no evidence whatsoever. Aaron figured (correctly) the midpoint of that range, two and a quarter million dollars, and exclaimed, "That's way too much." We agreed.

Fuerth, on the other hand, had suggested zero. "Well, I think Maria deserves *something*," I said.

"Particularly since she isn't getting any other kind of economic damages, like Don's lost wages," added another juror. Everyone else was on board.

Because we'd heard no evidence regarding the value of the chores Don did for his mother, we had to create our own. A bunch of backyard-less apartment dwellers— Aaron hasn't yet moved into his newly purchased suburban house—who call the super when something needs to be fixed, we were flying blind. Somehow, we came up with six thousand dollars a year. But by how many years should we multiply that amount? No one could remember Maria's life expectancy, so Aaron wrote the judge his second note.

This time, we were called into the courtroom for Mendez's response. "The jury has sent in a note, which has been marked court exhibit two hundred and sixty-five." Aaron blanched upon learning that his notes would become part of the official record. Was his handwriting sloppy, or did he spell something wrong, or cross stuff out? I wondered. Mendez continued. "The note reads as follows: 'Dear Judge Mendez, We are asking for the life expectancy of Maria Leo.' Maria Leo has a life expectancy of thirty-two point six years. You may continue to deliberate."

We all filed out. What a rigmarole for the procurement of a number, I thought.

When we got back to the jury room, Tony teased Aaron about the salutation in his note.

" 'Dear Judge Mendez, Pretty please could we have . . .'."

Is *that* why Aaron had looked embarrassed? "How *should* he address him?" I asked Tony. " 'Hey, Manuel'? Or 'Hey, Manny'?"

"How about, 'Yo, Judge!' " offered Aisha.

After we stopped laughing, Aaron grumbled, "Okay, okay. Next time I'll skip the salutation."

We ended up awarding Maria about two hundred thousand dollars for lost in-kind services from her son.

* * *

The next question contained our first big-ticket item. *Question #12A: "State the amount awarded for the emotional pain and suffering [aka pre-impact terror] Donald Christopher Leo endured between the moment he realized that he was about to be gravely injured or die and the moment he sustained a physical injury."*

Wait, I thought: Don's fear didn't necessarily end when he was injured. Then I told myself, "Don't go down that rabbit hole again: Just accept the Court's definition and answer the question."

To figure the amount of this type of award, we jurors first needed to agree on the earliest point at which Don could have been injured.

"Does anyone believe Dr. Schwartz's claim that Don injured his arms and legs while bracing himself in the cab?" one of the jurors asked.

"Not me," someone replied.

"But the cab did rock a little before it fell off," I said, "so Don could have hurt himself then."

"Well, Fuerth's expert, Fijalkowski, said Don wasn't injured until the cab hit the building across the street," another juror reminded us.

Eventually, we agreed that Don's pre-impact fear began when the cab started to wobble, and ended when it hit the apartment building across the street. But how long did that take? Of course, no one remembered the relevant witnesses' estimates accurately, so Aaron wrote another note.

Once again, we were summoned back into the courtroom for the answers. The low end of the estimates was fifteen seconds; the high end was five minutes. When the judge finished reading back the related testimony, he looked at his watch and told us it was time to go home.

Even at this point, with deliberations already begun, he warned us not only to avoid discussing the case with outsiders, but even with one another. (We can do this *only* in the jury room.) "I'll see you tomorrow at nine-thirty *sharp*," Mendez proclaimed.

Now that he could spy the post-trial Promised Land, even the typically patient judge was in a hurry.

* * *

After my family went to bed tonight, I sat in my living room and considered Question #12A, the one about Don Leo's pre-impact terror. I was relieved I could mull it over alone, for as long as I needed, without five sets of eyes peering at me in the jury room.

Based on the testimony that Judge Mendez had reread this afternoon, I estimated that Don suffered pre-impact fear for thirty seconds. Now the hard part: What was that worth?

Before I assigned a value, I tried to imagine what half a minute of terror would feel like. Have I ever feared for my own life?

There's that time I was mugged. It was around eleven o'clock on a steamy Manhattan summer night. I was getting home late because this was "closing week" at the magazine, when everything had to be finalized before going to the printer. As usual, all the editors wanted to make last-minute changes—some of them huge, like pulling a story and replacing it with a new one.

I stood on my apartment building's stoop, bleary-eyed, rummaging in my bag for my keys. There was a full moon, but the extra light it shed didn't help. I could ring the bell and ask my roommate to let me in, I thought, but she's probably already asleep.

I felt a hand cover my mouth. "I've got a gun," my assailant mumbled, poking me in the back. "Give me your money." I remained oddly calm, probably because the "weapon" hidden under his shirt felt more like the end of a finger. I pulled my wallet out of my purse and handed it back to him.

As I watched the mugger run away, I yelled, "Can you drop the wallet and keep just the cash?" I didn't want the hassle of having to replace my driver's license and credit cards, plus my wallet contained some precious family photos. Of course, he kept running, disappearing into the darkness of Riverside Park. Did I really think he was going to say, "Sure, miss, I'll place your wallet on top of this mailbox for you?" Naïve twenty-six-year-old that I was.

How about that mammogram I had about five years ago, after which the frowning technician asked me to wait for a doctor who would "speak to me further"? I had expected a death sentence, but it turned out I needed just an additional test, which revealed no cancer.

* * *

The best I could come up with were two incidents when I feared for my *children's* lives.

There was that time when Jules tumbled out of her stroller because of a particularly steep curb cut between the sidewalk and the street. My bewildered three-year-old, who had been asleep, awoke to find herself in the gutter. As I scooped her up while an oncoming car swerved around us, I told Jules, "Oh my God! I should have made sure you were belted in tight."

I folded the stroller, slung its carrying strap over my shoulder, and carried Jules the rest of the way home.

When James was five, I remembered, he was pushed off the top of a particularly high playground slide by his preschool nemesis. I shrieked in fury as I watched James fall, seemingly in slow-motion, and ran over to try to catch him. I missed, but thankfully James landed on soft sand and merely had the wind knocked out of him.

Strange, I thought, how both of these incidents, as in Don Leo's case, involved falls.

Then I dug deeper into my past and recalled my mother's first heart attack. As she sat on our family-room sofa, pale, gasping for breath, sweating, and shaking, my twelve-year-old self—my father was at work—called emergency. I was terrified that my mother would die before the ambulance arrived, but she survived. (A second heart attack killed her four years later.)

So, what is half a minute of terror—about the same amount of time I'd been scared out of my wits when my children fell, but less than the amount of time I feared my mom might die—worth? If, God forbid, the terror I'd felt had ended in their deaths, *no* amount of money would have sufficed. But in this instance, I couldn't think that way. I had to keep my end of the jury-duty bargain. I had to provide a value in dollars and cents.

I started with a low number and counted my way up until it felt right. A thousand dollars? A hundred thousand? Five hundred thousand? A million? Stop, that was enough. I came up with the following formula: Half a minute of terror equals one million dollars.

* * *

Even though it was premature, I figured, why stop here? (At this point, I thought, I'm not going to be able to sleep well anyway.) I might as well try the same exercise on "pain and suffering."

When have I been in agony? I've never broken a bone, partly because of luck, and partly because I'm not exactly a thrill seeker. (There was that time I tried downhill skiing, to impress a boyfriend, but I never really took to it.) Of course, I shouldn't forget the chronic pain I experienced in my twenties, caused by a jaw disorder. But that couldn't compare with the raw agony of an injury.

How about childbirth? It was torture, for sure, but for a good cause—birth, not death.

When I realized how fortunate I've been when it comes to pain and suffering, I started to feel guilty for never having appreciated my outsized good luck. After wallowing in shame for a minute or two, I returned to the task at hand, and took the easy way out.

I decided that half a minute of pain and suffering, like half a minute of fear, equaled one million dollars.

After playing God, I went to bed.

July 28

We got back to business at nine-thirty on the dot.

Don's pre-impact terror, we jurors agreed, lasted about half a minute. This conclusion, thankfully, jibed with my private calculations from last night.

Then we reviewed the dollar amounts suggested by the attorneys to compensate for Don's fear. Fuerth had proposed three hundred thousand for the *total* of his pre-impact terror *and* his pain and suffering, which he had estimated lasted no more than twenty-five seconds. Panzella had suggested thirty to forty million for that total, which she claimed lasted twenty-seven minutes.

"Okay," said Aaron, "let's halve these amounts to correspond with the first, pre-impact terror, part of the collapse. Half of Fuerth's suggestion is one hundred and fifty thousand; half of Panzella's suggestion is seventeen and a half million."

"Fuerth's proposal is way too low," I said, "and Panzella's is way too high."

Everyone agreed.

"So, what *is* a fair amount?" asked Aaron. "Should we discuss it?"

We stared at one another.

Martha said, "Well, I already have a figure in mind."

I guess the others had also reflected on this question last night, because they'd already decided, too.

"Okay, then. Let's go around the room," Aaron suggested.

We stared at one another again.

"I'll go first," I muttered. "One million."

I waited for the others to drop their jaws in unison, which they did, but not for the reason I was expecting.

"Ten million," countered Martha.

"I agree with ten million," said Aaron.

Eight million is the figure that came out of the mouths of Tony, Sandra, and Aisha.

I couldn't believe it: They thought my suggestion was too *low*.

How could they possibly think that thirty seconds of *anything*—even thirty seconds in the dreadful circles of Dante's inferno—was worth eight or ten million dollars?

I didn't ask.

Why not? I think I'd fallen prey to the phenomenon of "groupthink," the practice of making decisions in a way that discourages individual dissent. Not because someone had bullied me; in fact, if one of the jurors had done so, I probably would have made a stink. Rather, I stayed mum because I liked my fellow jurors so much that I didn't want to make waves.

Furthermore, I concluded that my midnight musings had been needless. No one had asked *me* to play God. I'd simply been asked to decide between the only opinions we'd been given on the matter, Fuerth's and Panzella's. *They* were the ones who'd been asked to play God.

The other jurors, I realized, may simply have chosen amounts that were roughly halfway between Fuerth's and Panzella's suggestions, a supremely sensible solution.

Or perhaps they were indulging in some "jury nullification," awarding Don's estate money for the forty-five years or so of life of which he had been deprived, rather than for the few seconds of fear he had experienced.

Or maybe they'd decided that after sitting through an

eleven-month trial, they were going to make their time mean something.

Or possibly they hated Mr. Lomma so much that they wanted to take him down big-time.

In any case, just as I had refrained from any attempt to change their minds, they also refrained from any attempt to change mine.

"What do we do now?" Aisha asked.

"Let's average these six numbers," suggested Tony, "and make that our award."

Again, Tony had come up with a great solution. What's more, my vote would, at the very least, bring the resulting award down slightly.

This time, perhaps because it was a huge amount of money, we all pulled out our smartphones to do the calculation. The result: Seven and a half million dollars.

As I wrote this tonight, I wondered why none of us had brought up practical considerations, such as the negative effects of this extremely high award on the construction industry, including higher building costs and insurance premiums. But what do two cops, one designer, one dispatcher (this is Aisha, who quit her stock-clerk job to work for a car service), one retired therapist, and one stay-at-home mother know or care about such matters?

Anyway, we'd gotten through our first "sixty-four-dollar question" with just a modicum of fuss.

* * *

Question #12B: "*State the amount awarded for the pain and suffering Donald Christopher Leo endured from the moment of physical injury to the moment of death.*"

To calculate the duration of Don's physical pain and suffering, Aaron wrote a note requesting a review of all testimony regarding the total amount of time it took the crane to collapse, from which we would subtract thirty seconds—the time Don experienced pre-impact fear. "I'd also like to ask for Don's autopsy report," Aaron said. Likely to satisfy our morbid curiosity, rather than any deliberative need, we agreed to this additional request.

After the judge reread the relevant testimony, we decided that Don had experienced thirty-five seconds of pain and suffering, five seconds longer than his pre-impact fear. Once again, it struck me as ridiculous that we had to dissect the accident to the level of seconds, but this is what the Court had asked of us.

While discussing Question #12B, we passed around Don's autopsy report. As I waited for my turn, I wondered how I'd react to the sight of Don's dead body. Over my lifetime, I've probably seen hundreds of photos of corpses in the media. But those were strangers, so I gave them a cursory look, experienced a tinge of repulsion, and moved on to the next headline. Don, while not a loved one, or even a friend, *did* feel like an acquaintance. I expected I'd feel *something*.

"I thought there'd be photos from different angles," Aaron said matter-of-factly as he passed the report on to Tony, his fellow battle-hardened cop. He gave it a quick look, and then it was Martha's turn. She shook her head in silence as she lingered over it.

When the folder reached my hands, I recalled the one dead body I've seen *in person*, twenty-six years ago. It was that of my father, as he lay in a casket opened just for immediate family members. Of course, that experience was infinitely more upsetting than this one: Here lay my own father, in that garish makeup that morticians apply in a lame attempt to make the dead look less dead. When I saw Daddy in that pitiful state, I had to look away after only a second or two.

Upon opening Don's autopsy report, my eyes were able to rest on the image for a couple of minutes. The photo showed Don's face only—no severed neck, no crushed skull. Its drained-of-blood flesh was white, unmarked (I'd expected deep gashes), and extremely swollen. Don's eyes and mouth were closed—did I think they'd be wide open, revealing an expression of horror like that of the face in Edvard Munch's painting *The Scream?* In any case, it was a far cry from the handsome portrait Panzella had displayed at the beginning of the trial.

Turning past the photo, I scrolled through the many annotated injuries suffered by this six-foot-two, three-hundred-and-twelve-pound thirty-year-old. Then I lit upon a remarkably detailed, poignant description of the clothes Don was wearing when he died: torn T-shirt; black, brief-style underwear; two socks; one sneaker (I guess the other one fell off and was lost in the debris); and a pair of jeans.

In Don's pockets were two paychecks from Sorbara dated May 29, 2008, one for regular pay, and one for overtime; a parking receipt; and two lengths of rope tied together. What, I wondered, was the significance of the latter? Was their function purely practical, part of the crane's cable; or were they symbolic, one length representing Don, and the other representing Janine, who would have been tied to Don in matrimony in just a few weeks? I wanted to believe that this was the correct interpretation, and sighed as I passed the report to Sandra.

When everyone had had a chance to look at the autopsy, one of the jurors brought us back to the task at hand.

"So, what do you guys think? Is pain worth more than fear, or vice versa, or are they worth the same?" our colleague asked.

"I don't see how we can distinguish the two," I replied.

Someone opined, "Mental anguish *can* be stronger than physical pain. That's why emotionally-disturbed people cut themselves, to distract themselves from their destructive thoughts."

"Yeah, but if I had to choose between someone scaring me and someone hurting me, I'd choose to be scared every time," countered another juror.

In the end, we decided that the two feelings are equal in awfulness, and thus equal in value.

The only thing we *could* assess adequately was the factual difference: the length of time that Don felt physical pain and suffering, about five seconds longer than he felt fear. Using our seven-and-a-half million pre-impact fear award as our "building block," we unanimously agreed that eight million dollars seemed about right for this slightly longer period of suffering.

* * *

Finally, we got to the questions regarding punitive damages. Are they warranted against James F. Lomma, New York Crane, and J.F. Lomma, Inc.?

Since we'd already agreed that all three's actions were "reckless and wanton," it went without saying, we believed, that punitive damages were appropriate. All six of us speedily signed our names to "Yes" regarding each of these defendants. We weren't asked to provide an amount for punitive damages, and I assumed that meant it would be decided by someone else—the judge, or possibly another jury. I was relieved to be absolved of this responsibility.

The verdict sheets for the estate of Donald Christopher Leo ended with the following directive: "Proceed no further. Stop and tell the court officer that you have reached a verdict, and return it to the courtroom."

Aaron knocked on the door, and Melanie gave him Ramadan's verdict sheets in exchange for Don's.

I wondered, will Melanie, the judge, and/or the lawyers take a peek at our verdict for Don? Or will they wait until we deliver our verdict for Ramadan?

* * *

Around one o'clock, Melanie brought us pizza, today's lawyer-funded lunch. We sated our considerable appetites—rendering a verdict, it turns out, burns *a lot* of calories—and then turned our attention to the recently-delivered Q & A for Ramadan Kurtaj.

We flew through questions one through eight, which were identical to those on Don's verdict sheets, and were all related to liability. We answered them the same way we had for Don.

* * *

Question nine, regarding Ramadan's pre-impact terror damages, brought us to a halt. In her closing, Karten had proposed ten million dollars, while Fuerth had made no suggestion whatsoever for pre-impact fear.

"I'd really like to know how Ramadan's parents and Selvi are going to share the money," said Tony.

"Me, too," I replied, "but I doubt they'll tell us."

Nevertheless, Aaron wrote the judge a note. "It's worth a try," he shrugged.

As expected, Mendez replied that he could not divulge this information.

"Okay, so let's talk about it," said Aaron. "How long did Ramadan fear for his life?"

"He obviously became aware of the danger after Don did," replied one juror.

"Yes, but Don's fear ended before Ramadan's did," added another. "Don's ended when the crane hit the building across the street, but Ramadan's didn't end until he was pinned under the cab."

"I think their fear lasted about the same amount of time," I said.

Everyone agreed, and we awarded Ramadan seven and a half million dollars, the same amount we had awarded Don.

To determine the award for Ramadan's post-impact pain and suffering, we requested the testimony of the EMT who had treated him in the ambulance, plus the report from the medical examiner. (There was no autopsy report for us to look at because Ramadan's family had declined this procedure for religious reasons.)

"Does anybody think Ramadan regained consciousness after he was intubated?" asked Aaron.

"Are you wondering about the seven out of ten he got on that coma scale?" I asked.

Aaron nodded yes.

"I think it was a mistake," replied another juror.

"I agree," I said. "I don't see how he could have recovered that level of consciousness after all those meds they'd given him."

For once, all of us concurred with Fuerth, who had estimated that Ramadan was conscious for thirty-six minutes, from the time he became aware of the collapse to the time he entered the ER.

Fuerth had valued these thirty-six minutes of pain at two and a half million dollars. Karten, who naturally believed that the coma scale notation was *not* a mistake and that Ramadan had suffered much longer, had suggested twenty-five million.

All six of us sat in silence for several minutes, in private struggle for a solution.

I'd already rejected the formula I'd devised in my living room last night—that thirty seconds of pain and suffering were worth one million dollars—when I'd agreed to award Don eight million dollars for thirty-five seconds of this type of distress. I needed a new formula, one that would correlate Don's and Ramadan's awards for pain and suffering, just as their awards for pre-impact terror had been correlated. That was the only fair way to do it, I believed.

But when I figured that would mean an award of about half a *billion* dollars in pain and suffering for Ramadan, I realized how unworkable such a correlation would be.

Then, I thought, what if we award the midpoint in the range between Fuerth's and Karten's suggestions? This would be eleven and a quarter million dollars. That was too little: How could we in good conscience give Ramadan just over eleven million for more than half an hour of pain and suffering when we'd given Don eight million for thirty-five seconds' worth?

"How about we award Ramadan triple what we awarded Don, which would be twenty-four million dollars?" someone suggested.

"I like it," replied Tony.

"It's starting to feel like Monopoly money," commented Martha jadedly.

"I agree, it *is* an absurd amount of money," said Aaron. "But does anyone have a better idea?"

There were no takers. Eventually, everyone was on board.

As I wrote this tonight, I was still haunted by the nagging sense that twenty-four million, while an enormous sum, was too little in comparison with Don's award. If I could, I would go back in time and lower my award for Don to align it with the amount I thought right for Ramadan. I felt better, however, when I realized that if Don's and Ramadan's cases had been tried separately, and decided by two different juries, no one would ever have expected the damages to be correlated.

* * *

The next two questions asked us to determine economic damages for Ramadan's parents and for his widow. To answer them, we needed to review the reports of the actuaries representing both sides regarding Ramadan's projected earnings; Uke's and Selvi's testimony about the support Ramadan gave them while he was alive; and Ramadan's parents' and widow's life expectancies.

We gave Ramadan's parents a little more than four hundred thousand dollars, about a quarter of the two million Karten had suggested in her closing, but only twice the amount Fuerth had proposed.

For Selvi, Karten had suggested five and a quarter million dollars, and Fuerth had suggested no more than three million.

"I don't think Ramadan gave Selvi a penny after she left

him, and I don't think she deserves a penny [in economic damages] now," declared Aaron.

"I feel the same way," said Aisha.

"But the judge said Ramadan was legally obligated to support his wife," I reminded them. "So even though I agree that he gave her nothing before he died, we *have* to give her something now."

In the end, we threw Fuerth a bone, awarding Selvi less than even he had proposed: just eighty thousand dollars.

We quickly answered the last three questions, awarding punitive damages against Lomma individually, New York Crane, and J.F. Lomma, Inc., just as we had for Don.

Then Aaron knocked on the door for the last time.

We were ready for our big moment.

We entered the courtroom to announce both verdicts.

* * *

I felt even more nervous than I had on our very first day.

To distract myself from my trembling hands and queasy stomach, I scrutinized the lawyers, trying to read their thoughts. Panzella looked shell-shocked. Karten looked manic. O'Neill looked calm. Fuerth looked blank. Williams looked resigned. Slattery looked confident. Fumo looked pale.

Then I took in the audience. On the plaintiffs' side, Maria Leo, who wore all black, as if newly in mourning for Don, sat between her only living son, Shawn, and her daughter, Jessica, clutching their hands. Uke Kurtaj's head was lowered near his lap, as if he were afraid of a second disappointing verdict. Selvi Sinanovic was actually paying attention. Kayla, Alison, and Erin, three of the "retired" jurors, sat excitedly in the back row. (I resisted the temptation to wave.) I thought Shawn might be with them, but, for some reason, he still hadn't been released from solitary.

On the defendants' side, Mr. and Mrs. Sorbara, plus Mr. Muirhead (Brady Marine's president), looked apprehensive. Mr. Lomma was still AWOL.

Everyone else in the audience, which was full, was a blur. I did notice, however, that for the first time an armed guard was standing between the gallery and the well of the courtroom. It had never occurred to me that someone might react violently to our verdict. Even though this precaution seemed excessive, it made me even more nervous. A second guard was positioned next to the judge.

There was another newbie in the courtroom, who stood between the lawyers and the judge and faced the jury. The only thing I could remember about this woman, whose sole job was to read the verdict sheets' questions aloud to Aaron, our foreman, is that her pedicured feet were clad in flip-flops. They struck me as overly casual, especially on verdict day.

She asked Aaron to stand. As he delivered our first set of answers, putting liability squarely on the shoulders of Lomma and his companies, Fuerth continued to look down at his binder, revealing no emotion. Williams raised her eyes periodically, her lips pursed.

When we absolved Sorbara and Brady Marine, Slattery

looked jubilant, Fumo looked relieved, and their clients looked overjoyed.

When Aaron stated that Don Leo was zero percent at fault for the accident, his mother collapsed into her remaining children's arms, as if a huge weight had been lifted off her weary body. Tears ran down her face, and when I looked at her, she mouthed, "Thank you."

When we announced our damages, the plaintiffs' lawyers looked ecstatic, and their clients looked stunned.

When we declared that punitive damages were warranted, Fuerth lowered his head even farther.

When Aaron, who had fulfilled his role with dignity, retook his seat in the jury box, he turned around and flashed a big smile at the three of us in the back row.

I was expecting Melanie's "All rise" directive, but instead the judge uttered the following: "Additional evidence has to be submitted to the jurors for them to properly assess the amount of punitive damages that is to be awarded in both cases."

What? That was our job, too? I felt like our erstwhile jury room pumpkin, like I was going to explode.

"We cannot do that now," Mendez continued, as I wrapped my head around the fact that the trial *still* wasn't over. "We will adjourn at this point and reconvene Thursday."

* * *

Tonight, I told Bob that my stint as a juror wasn't over yet. "It turns out *we're* the ones who have to determine punitive damages," I complained. "I never expected we'd have to do that, too."

"The judge probably decided not to give you a heads-up because it might have motivated you to hurry through your first verdict," Bob replied.

"Well, it went pretty fast, anyway."

"Or it could have influenced you to reject punitive damages altogether, just to get the trial over with."

"We're not that desperate. We still have *some* principles."

July 30

There was a brownout in the courthouse today.

With sputtering air conditioning and dimmed lights, our jury room felt like a murky swamp. Likewise running on reduced energy, we jurors draped ourselves on the table like wet rags.

* * *

In the courtroom, Fuerth and Williams sat alone on the defense's side of the aisle, now that Slattery's and Fumo's clients had been exonerated. This team's new task was to keep our punitive damages as low as possible, and their primary strategy was to plead poverty.

"Mr. Lomma and his companies are not as rich as you might think," Fuerth began, "or as wealthy as the plaintiffs' lawyers will claim they are." To bolster this assertion, Fuerth put into evidence a selection of twenty-seven tax returns from 2006 to 2014, some for James Lomma individually, some for J.F. Lomma, Inc., and some for New York Crane. "More returns are on their way from my office, and they should be here soon," Fuerth assured us.

Gee, I thought, he's had only eleven months to get these ducks in a row. Is it possible Fuerth was surprised by our decision to award punitive damages, and that's why he wasn't fully prepared?

While I slumped in my seat at the dreary prospect of reviewing a stack of tax documents, Fuerth interpreted select figures for us. "From his personal returns," Fuerth stated, "you can see that Mr. Lomma's average annual income is only one million four hundred thousand dollars." *Only?* He's a one percenter!

Fuerth went on to suggest that we award half this annual average—seven hundred thousand dollars—to Don's estate, and the same amount to Ramadan's. "That's taking a year of personal income away from Mr. Lomma, no meager amount," stressed Fuerth.

He then proposed that we award half of the average annual earnings of J.F. Lomma, Inc.—three hundred and fifty thousand dollars—and half of New York Crane's 2009 earnings—two hundred and fifty thousand dollars—to each estate. (Fuerth magnanimously chose 2009 alone, rather than an average of several years, because in the others New York Crane had earned zero or incurred a loss.)

In total, Fuerth was recommending one million three hundred thousand dollars for Don, and the same total for Ramadan, in punitive damages. "These amounts are minimal in comparison with your compensatory damages,"

Fuerth conceded. "But those are so high that they are punitive in and of themselves." And *any* amount of punitive damages, he insisted, would stigmatize his client. Finally, begged Fuerth, "Don't put Mr. Lomma's companies out of business."

Fuerth finished before lunch, and this time our free meal was a selection of limp, pre-made sandwiches from a grocery store. Perhaps Fuerth, whose client finds himself in newly-straightened circumstances, had an outsized influence on today's choice, I thought. With no deliberating yet to be done, we ate fast, then returned to the courtroom to hear the plaintiffs' lawyers' take on Lomma's fortunes.

* * *

As portended by Fuerth, O'Neill, who spoke for the Kurtaj estate, claimed Lomma is actually very wealthy. "No matter your award, this guy isn't gonna end up on food stamps," O'Neill assured us, after which Tony leaned back in his seat and guffawed.

"Don't be fooled by the tax returns. The tax laws are created in such a way that someone like Lomma can make a great deal of money," O'Neill explained, "but show little in taxable income.

"For example, take a look at Lomma's individual return for 2006," O'Neill continued. "Lomma's wages are relatively low, but this is deceptive: Wealthy people like to underpay themselves, because they prefer to get their money in the form of capital gains, which are taxed at a much lower rate." Then there's Lomma's interest income:

"He lists one hundred and seventy thousand dollars. You have to have millions to earn that much interest."

As for Lomma's companies, much of their income is sheltered by equipment depreciation, claimed O'Neill. "And in a not-so-strange coincidence, Lomma appears to have purposely reduced his businesses' revenues since the 2008 accident. He knew a civil lawsuit was inevitable, so he tried to shield his companies from any damages he might eventually have to pay."

O'Neill went on to explain that there must be a correlation between the amount of our punitive damages and the amount of the compensatory damages we've already awarded. "I propose five dollars of punitive damages for every one dollar of compensatory [economic and noneconomic] damages," he told us.

He was wise to deliver his suggestion in this fashion: Five dollars for every one dollar at first seemed reasonable. But when I remembered that we'd awarded the Kurtaj estate a total of thirty-seven and a half million dollars in compensatory damages, O'Neill's recommendation came to more than one hundred and eighty-seven million, a staggering sum. There was no way I'd award that much, I thought.

* * *

O'Neill ended, just as Karten had in her closing statement before our first verdict, with a rousing call for us jurors to be heroes.

"Yesterday, you gave a verdict for the families of the victims," O'Neill declared. "Today, I'm asking you to give a verdict for the community." (Sounds great, I wanted to interject, but how come you and your client, and not "the community," get this money?[3]) "Today you have an opportunity to do what the district attorney, in the criminal trial, was unable to do." This statement made me wonder: If the D.A. *had* put Lomma behind bars, would we still have voted for punitive damages? Or would we have considered prison to have been punishment enough?

"You have an opportunity, collectively, to make a difference," O'Neill continued. "You have an opportunity to change the way the business of construction is conducted in New York.

"Your verdict is your legacy," proclaimed O'Neill. "Your verdict gives meaning to the eleven months you have sat here and endured a trial that has gone on long enough. From the bottom of my heart, I thank you, and God bless you."

I wasn't sure I wanted "Here lieth Cynthia M. Pigott, who changed the way the business of construction is conducted in New York" inscribed on my tombstone. But I had to admit that O'Neill's *was* an eloquent summation.

* * *

Thankfully, Panzella's presentation on behalf of the Leo estate was uncharacteristically brief. She began by reminding us that, before the Ninety-First Street accident,

---

3 After the trial ended, I discovered that some jurisdictions *do* require punitive damages to be shared with state coffers.

the City had ordered Lomma to take four other Kodiak cranes out of service, because they too had been poorly maintained. "This man is going to keep on doing business this way unless you make him stop," Panzella exclaimed.

To reveal how rich Lomma is, Panzella skipped the tax returns. "Mr. O'Neill is much better at that than I am," she conceded. She took a different tack: "Lomma owns three hundred and eighty cranes," Panzella began. "If each crane averages thirty-five thousand dollars in monthly rental income, three hundred and eighty of them have the potential to earn Lomma more than thirteen million dollars a month," she continued. "It's been eighty-six months since Don and Ramadan perished, a period of time during which Lomma's cranes, at a rental rate of seventy percent, could have earned almost eight hundred million dollars.

"That's the kind of money you're looking at," Panzella concluded, conveniently excluding overhead, labor costs, and the like from her sky-high total. Like O'Neill, Panzella asked for five times our compensatory damages, which would be about seventy-five million for the Leo estate.

When Panzella finished, Judge Mendez told us we'd been ordered to evacuate the building because of the brownout. "I can't give you my charge on punitive damages as I had intended," he said regretfully. "I'll have to wait until tomorrow to deliver those instructions."

We jurors heaved a collective sigh. What was one more day, on top of the one hundred and twenty-five we'd already been cooped up at Sixty Centre Street?

July 31

In his charge on punitive damages, the judge told us we should consider the following in determining our award, which, he reminded us, must be correlated to our compensatory damages: whether Mr. Lomma and his companies' conduct demonstrated (a) an indifference to, or reckless disregard of, the health, safety, or rights of others; (b) improper motive or vindictiveness; (c) outrageous or oppressive intentionality; and (d) efforts to cover up the bad behavior.

We should also take into account, instructed Mendez, (a) the extent to which Lomma's and his companies' conduct affected third parties; (b) whether or not Lomma and his companies had committed similar acts in the past; and (c) the effect our award will have on Lomma's and his companies' financial condition.

* * *

I wish I could say the jury carefully parsed each consideration (although the first one went without saying, since without it we wouldn't have awarded punitive damages in the first place). We didn't. Instead, we zeroed in on the last consideration, the most tangible one—Lomma's and his companies' financial condition—and skipped the rest.

To that end, Melanie lugged towering stacks of tax returns into our jury room and dumped them on the table. Aaron divided them into six piles, and we dove in.

After a few minutes, I confessed, "I don't really understand what I'm looking at, or what I should be looking for."

"I think we're wasting our time," added another juror.

"Well, they gave us these returns for a reason," Aaron replied. "Let's give it a try."

We made a good-faith effort at dissecting the returns, scrawling figures in our notebooks, adding and multiplying (accurately, I hope) on our smartphones, trying to determine each entity's average annual income and any other relevant information we could glean.

By the end of the day, I surrendered. "I'd need a tax accountant to help me make sense of these documents."

Martha added, "These numbers don't come close to revealing their subjects' true net worth."

Blank looks enveloped our exhausted faces. Everyone agreed the exercise seemed fruitless.

"Let's rest over the weekend and see if we can figure something out on Monday," said Aaron.

August 3

I'm not proud to admit it: This morning, all the jurors agreed, come hell or high water, that this was it. We were at the end of our ropes. We had to finish today.

We spent another couple of hours wrestling with the tax returns. "What should we do, Aaron?" Aisha pleaded.

"We're still getting nowhere," Sandra groaned.

Someone, I don't remember who, suggested each estate get the same amount in punitive damages that we'd given

Ramadan for his pain and suffering: twenty-four million dollars. Once more, it struck each of us as a worthy compromise—not too low, and not too high—and it complied with the rule to correlate our punitive award with our compensatory award.

Aaron knocked on the door. Melanie escorted us to the courtroom, this time for the very last time.

After Aaron announced our verdict, I noticed that no one—neither the lawyers for the plaintiffs, nor those for the defendants—looked happy. What do they want from us? I wondered. Could have been better, but could have been worse, for both sides. Their apparent ingratitude stung, and I was wishing them all good riddance as we jurors stood up to leave.

As we neared the exit, we heard some intermittent clapping behind us, then a crescendo of applause. "Turn around," Melanie urged us. Everyone in the courtroom was standing and grinning, even the losers, Fuerth and Williams. First Judge Mendez, then Karten, Panzella, and Fuerth gave speeches of gratitude. In one fell swoop, their words erased not only the aggravation I had felt just a few minutes before, but even the accumulated aggravations of the past year.

We deserved this standing ovation, I thought. Ours *was* a heroic performance. We'd nailed the bad guy, who will have to cough up a lot of dough to compensate the plaintiffs for the horrific loss of their loved ones. And even though I wasn't so sure I wanted this to be my "legacy," we *did* help rescue our fellow New Yorkers from further construction catastrophes through our punitive damage award.

Best of all, we'd brought the longest trial in Manhattan history to a close.

* * *

Judge Mendez invited us to descend from the jury box to join the lawyers and the audience members, who also moved to the well of the courtroom. We mingled like acquaintances at a cocktail party. I call them "acquaintances," even though we've been with them for the past eleven months, because we've observed one another without knowing one another, like zoo animals watched from a safe distance.

Just as I had at the start of the trial, I felt like I was acting in a movie. Or maybe a play. Think Theater of the Absurd.

As I made my way among the "players," Fuerth stopped me to make a final plea for pity. "My firm's nickname for this case was 'Dead Man Walking'," he told me.

I stopped O'Neill to confide, "My husband just remembered that you and he were on opposite sides of a lawsuit several years ago." (Bob and I had agreed that it was *way* too late to tell the judge about his third link to the trial—the first being his connection to the firm that represented the general contractor, the second being his friendship with Mendez's boss.)

Karten stopped me to announce, "All the lawyers used you as our jury sounding board, because your face is so expressive."

I stopped Williams to tell her, "You handled yourself well, considering this was your first trial."

Mrs. Leo stopped me to say, "Every day I worried that you jurors would suddenly decide not to show up."

The "party" wound down, and it was time to go. On our way back to the jury room, I spied a trash can spilling over with our shredded notebooks, our scribblings lost forever. "I never wrote a single word in mine," Tony told me proudly, pointing to his head and the fine memory inside.

We gave Melanie a couple of presents: a crystal vase, picked out by Martha, and a selfie, framed by me, of the seven remaining jurors standing at the top of Sixty Centre Street's majestic staircase (reproduced on this book's back cover). Melanie shook her head and teared up as she opened each one.

Then Judge Mendez entered and told us, once again, how grateful he was for our steadfastness. His thanks did not seem over the top to me: After almost a year, Mendez's bosses would likely have been extremely displeased if he'd lost so many jurors that the case had ended in a mistrial. This time, *we* got a gift: a coffee mug with the seal of New York State on one side, and the words "New York County Juror" and "Juror Appreciation Week" on the other.

The judge also presented us with a diploma-like "Certificate of Appreciation," signed and sealed by his Honor. It was a hokey token, but I proudly showed it to my husband and kids when I got home.

Then we packed up for the last time, leaving behind the jigsaw puzzles for the room's next occupants. I hoped they wouldn't have as much time to work on them as we'd had.

* * *

"Before you leave, the New York County Clerk would like to see you," Melanie told us breathlessly, implying that such a meeting would be a big honor. Who the heck is that? I thought, until I remembered that he's the fellow whose signature is on every single jury-duty summons. Melanie led us to the first-floor office of Milton Tingling (yet another Dickensian name).

We took seats around an enormous conference table, whose surface, I noted, gleamed like a mirror, unlike the one in our jury room. Judge Tingling (I hadn't realized that this job required one to be a full-fledged judge) commended us for our service. "I would love it if all of you sat on more trials," he told us. "But I'll understand if you accept the offer of a lifetime exemption." He added, "I'm going to order a plaque with your names on it to display above my desk."

Shawn grinned, and whispered to me, "That would be so cool!"

As we rose to leave, Sandra nudged me. "I just realized, Tingling is the judge who performed my marriage ceremony at City Hall!"

"You should remind him," I urged her, but she demurred shyly.

None of us wanted to be interviewed by the press waiting out front, so Melanie escorted us through a maze of hallways and out a side door that I'd never known existed. She gave me a hug, which I had trouble returning because of her bulletproof vest. "I've got something to tell you before you go," Melanie said cryptically.

"Oh?" I answered.

"Remember how, when I took attendance at the beginning of *voir dire,* your name wasn't on my list?"

"Kind of."

"Your name was missing because you'd joined the wrong line in Room 452. If you'd gotten in the right line, you would have ended up in a *voir dire* for a different personal injury case that wrapped up in less than a week."

"Really? I hope fate led me to the wrong line for a reason."

Melanie smiled, then told me to visit any time.

* * *

Our group decided to make one last trip to our favorite watering hole. On the way, we were followed by Panzella and Karten, and I worried that they were headed to the same destination. Happily, by the time we got there, they'd disappeared. Our jury "family" could relax, without being spied on.

Tony asked, "Is it too early in the day to order pickle backs?" which has become our jury's signature drink.

"Nah," replied Aisha.

"Nobody's going to work this afternoon, right?" I asked.

"Nope," replied Aaron. "Drink up, everyone!"

We talked about getting back to our "real" lives.

"My fiancée is dreading it," said Aaron. "I have to admit, it's been nice getting home early every day, instead of working twelve-hour shifts."

"Yeah," agreed Tony. "But I *am* looking forward to overtime pay."

"I can't wait to get back to my studio," said Martha. "I already know what my first piece will be: I'm going to do an abstract painting based on Ed Cox's weld samples."

I didn't say much. As the reality of my "real" life sank in, I felt depressed.

I didn't want to go back to the life of a premature retiree. I could, I suppose, look for magazine work. But let's be real: Is anyone going to hire a fifty-five-year-old who's been out of the workforce for twenty years?

Not likely. It was a sobering realization.

* * *

After dinner tonight, I told Bob about my post–jury duty loss of "purpose."

"Why don't you volunteer at Jules's school?' Bob suggested.

"No thanks," I replied. "Been there, done that."

"Somewhere else, then. Maybe a museum?"

"Perhaps. I'll think about it," I lied.

"I've got it," Bob declared when he got home. "Why don't you write a book?"

"About what?" I replied.

"The trial. Write about everything you were dying to tell me, our families, our friends, and our neighbors, but couldn't. Now you're free to say whatever you like."

I mulled over Bob's idea. "I *did* write about my experience in my diary, so I've already got some material to work with."

"And while the trial may be over, the case isn't," added Bob. "Fuerth will definitely file an appeal. It could end up changing your verdict significantly."

"I could also get my hands on the 'puzzle pieces' that were missing in our trial, including the biggest one of all: a transcript of the criminal trial."

"It would be fascinating to find out how that ended in a totally different verdict."

"Who knows *what* I might find."

I didn't need any more convincing. This former juror decided to begin her next "duty" first thing tomorrow morning.

The Diary, Part Two

THE TRUTH
(September 2015–
November 2018)

NINE

THE WHOLE PICTURE BEHIND THE CIVIL TRIAL

September 28, 2015

How many facts, I wondered, had been hidden from the jury during Leo et al. v. Lomma et al.?

After I got a copy of the civil trial transcript, I zeroed in on all the hours of back-and-forth between the judge and the lawyers that had taken place outside the jury's presence. After counting more than fifty pages' worth of petty bickering among the attorneys (eliciting responses such as "Stop acting like kindergartners!" from the exasperated judge), I finally found answers to many of the questions that had dogged me during the trial. Answers that shined light on the real story behind the case.

My lawyer husband, Bob, led me to a second treasure trove of information: the New York County Supreme Court's website. With Bob's help, I combed through most of the supporting documents submitted in this case, and found yet more revealing answers.

* * *

How did Ramadan's parents and his widow share their award? Before the trial, it was decided that Ramadan's parents would get the first two hundred thousand dollars of any damages awarded to the Kurtaj estate (an amount so low, it suggests they never expected our award to be as high as it was). Anything above that amount, they agreed to split fifty-fifty with Selvi.

* * *

Why did the jury have to apportion liability among Lomma and his companies? Because of an obscure New York law that applies in personal injury cases with more than one defendant.[4] If the jury had found Lomma *less* than fifty percent liable, he would *not* have been required to cover J.F. Lomma's and New York Crane's *noneconomic* damages—if, and only if, the jury had also voted *not* to pierce the corporate veil. (Yes, it took me a while to figure out this complicated scenario!)

* * *

Why did the plaintiffs seem to be on the same side as defendants Sorbara and Brady Marine? Sorbara settled with the Kurtaj estate before we delivered our verdict, and Brady settled with both estates before the trial even started. The only reason these two parties remained until the

---

4 This law requires a defendant who is found *more than* fifty percent liable to cover the *noneconomic* damages of the other defendants.

proceeding's bitter end was because Lomma had claims against them, and they had claims against him. (In other words, Lomma told Sorbara and Brady, "If you're found liable, you owe me money." And Sorbara and Brady told Lomma, "If you're found liable, you owe us money.")

A lightbulb went off in my head: Brady's claim against Lomma explains why Williams, one of Lomma's attorneys, tried to blame Brady for the bad weld, even though her team's theory was that operator error had caused the accident.

These "secret" ongoing claims also explain why Slattery and Fumo put on their own witnesses regarding liability: They had to prove that they weren't liable *not* to the plaintiffs, but to Lomma. However, they didn't need to put on witnesses regarding damages, because they'd already paid the plaintiffs.

* * *

Why didn't Panzella examine the Sorbara witnesses? The Leo estate *never* sued Sorbara, because it opted to take workers' compensation instead.

* * *

How were matters resolved with the other defendants? The land owner was dismissed from the case soon after the trial started, which explains why their lawyer, Strugatz, disappeared early on. The developers and the general contractor settled with the Kurtaj estate in the middle of the trial, and later on the judge dismissed these parties from the Leo action. After that, the only reason *they* stuck around a while longer was because of various claims against one another.

* * *

By the end of the trial, the plaintiffs were actually suing *just* Lomma and his companies, and none of the other defendants. The jury had no idea.

November 7

I waited until Bob came home from the gym to unburden myself.

My review of the transcript had led to a totally unexpected development: It gave me second thoughts about our verdict. The verdict into which our jury had poured our hearts, souls, and almost a year of our lives. The verdict I'd been so proud of just a couple of months ago.

I *had* to tell Bob about my misgivings while he was still dripping in sweat.

"Let's start with the judge's instructions on punitive damages," I said, lugging the thick printout to the kitchen table. "He said they should be awarded for conduct that represents a *'high degree of immorality* [my italics].' One of the synonyms for 'immorality' in the dictionary is 'evil.' To my mind, 'evil' suggests intent. But Lomma did not set out to kill anyone."

"Of course, he didn't," Bob replied, grabbing a kitchen towel to dry himself off.

"Mendez also said that Lomma's actions had to demonstrate '*conscious* [my italics] indifference to and *utter* disregard of their effects on the health, safety, and rights of others.' 'Conscious' means 'with critical awareness,' and 'utter' means 'to the highest degree.' Was Lomma 'critically aware' that the crane was unsafe? If someone had said, 'You realize this crane could hurt or kill someone, right?', would Lomma have replied, 'Yes, but I don't care, I'm going to put it to work anyway?' And was his lack of regard 'to the highest degree,' or was he only vaguely aware of the danger?' "

"These are good questions."

"During deliberations, all we talked about was the meaning of 'reckless' and 'wanton.' Even though we never really understood what the latter meant, we agreed that Lomma had been reckless, which he *had* been. But I don't remember *ever* discussing the *degree* to which Lomma had been reckless, and whether or not his behavior met this high standard."

"So you think you *shouldn't* have awarded punitive damages?" asked Bob.

"I hate to admit it, but yes, I think we were wrong to do so," I replied, staring at my feet.

* * *

Bob headed toward the bathroom.

"Wait, there's more."

"A *second* second thought?"

"I'm afraid so. I'm also not so sure we were right to pierce the corporate veil. Mendez said that we had to satisfy three elements to do so. Let me read you the third element: 'The corporations' owner *used his complete control* [my italics] to commit a fraud, or a dishonest or unjust act, in violation of the injured parties' rights.' Lomma *himself* would have had to order the bad bearing to satisfy this element. He didn't. He ceded this control to his mechanic, Varganyi."

"If you did get these two questions wrong, it's not your fault," Bob assured me. "It's nuts that the jury didn't get the judge's instructions in *writing*, particularly since they were so long and complicated."

I reflected a moment, then added, "At least I still think the weld caused the accident. And that Lomma and his companies were the only ones to blame, even if I think we punished them too severely."

November 20

Were Lomma and his companies the only ones to blame?

During the trial, I'd always harbored the nagging belief that RTR, the Chinese company that actually manufactured the bearing with the defective weld, was primarily at fault for the accident.

Problem was, RTR wasn't on trial.

Why not? Because, I found out, the plaintiffs thought

it would be too much work to go after RTR. Apparently, lawsuits against foreign companies are a losing battle—extremely complicated and usually fruitless.

In effect, it would have been better for Lomma if the manufacturer had been located in the States: The plaintiffs more than likely *would* have sued an American company, and Lomma would have had someone to share the blame—and to help pay the damages.

* * *

Then there's the City: I'd always thought its Department of Buildings was at fault, too.

At the outset, I discovered, the plaintiffs *did* sue the City. But it was dismissed before the case went to trial. Here's what the judge who oversaw the case before Mendez ruled: "Governmental functions undertaken for the protection and safety of the public are generally immune from negligence claims, absent a special relationship between the injured parties and the government entity." This judge found that no such "special relationship" had been proven, so the City, like RTR, got off scot-free.

* * *

What if RTR and the City *had* been on trial? The jury would have had to apportion responsibility for the accident among the following: (a) RTR; (b) The City of New York; (c) Sorbara; (d) Brady Marine; (e) Don Leo; (f) James Lomma; (g) J.F. Lomma; and (h) New York Crane.

In the jury's percentage distribution of liability, I would have voted in the following manner:

RTR	50%
The City of New York	15%
Sorbara	0%
Brady Marine	0%
Don Leo	0%
James Lomma	25%
J.F. Lomma	5%
New York Crane	5%

It was a very different picture of who's to blame.

And it seemed a lot closer to the truth.

TEN

AN INSIGHT FROM THE 2012 CRIMINAL TRIAL

December 6

How can two different trials about the same two deaths lead to two opposite truths?

Reviewing the transcript of the 2012 criminal proceeding, I hoped to figure out how Lomma got off in that trial, but not in ours.

* * *

For starters, there's a higher standard of proof in a criminal trial than there is in a civil trial. In the former, it's "beyond a reasonable doubt," versus the latter's significantly lower "preponderance of evidence." From the get-go, Lomma had a leg up in the criminal trial.

* * *

What's more, the criminal defense team had an ace up its sleeve that Fuerth didn't have in the civil trial. In the criminal trial, an accident reconstructionist proved the operator-error theory of the collapse in a slick, easy-to-follow presentation. Fuerth had wanted this expert to testify in the civil trial, too, but Judge Mendez, who deemed this theory overly speculative, and unsupported by eyewitness testimony, ruled against him.

Remember the never-revealed, sheet-draped object Fuerth set up at the beginning of his defense? It was a scale model of the accident site that replicated the crane, the project under construction, and the apartment building across the street. In the criminal trial, the accident reconstructionist used this replica to make mathematical calculations proving that the crane *had to have* been operated in error.

Proven error number one: The crane *was* boomed too high, based on damage to the cooling tower on the roof of the apartment building across the street from the construction site. This tower was gashed by the falling crane boom because it was at an eighty-three-degree angle, five degrees higher than the limit mandated by the City's Department of Buildings (and higher even than the limit set in the crane's manual). If the angle had been lower, the boom would have missed the tower altogether during its descent.

Proven error number two: The crane's hoist line *was* raised too high, based on damage to the wheel through which this line was pulled. (The curved indentation on the wheel proved that it had been struck by the headache ball.)

* * *

Of course, Don Leo could have made these errors only if the safety devices had been disabled. The accident reconstructionist proved that, post-accident, the switches *were* indeed missing, as were the devices that would have secured them to the crane.

While the safeties might have fallen off during the collapse, the accident reconstructionist claimed that one of them had been protected by its position between the crane's rope drum and fuel tank, so damage due to the collapse was "unlikely." But he conceded that the other one *could* have been removed by falling debris.

* * *

Which is correct, the criminal trial's not-guilty verdict, or the civil trial's liable verdict?

Even though the proof presented by the prosecution in the criminal trial wasn't airtight, I can see how it might have planted 'reasonable doubt' in the mind of the judge. I think his not-guilty verdict was the right one.

However, I still think our verdict was correct, too. Even if the accident reconstructionist *had* testified in our trial, I think the 'preponderance of the evidence' would have led us to find Lomma liable.

* * *

My conclusion left me dispirited. If both verdicts are right, I thought, what's the point? Do they cancel each other out? Did I spend a year of my life on a fool's errand?

ELEVEN

ONE BIG REVEAL (AND TWO BIG ERRORS) IN THE CIVIL APPEAL

October 5, 2016

I found a bombshell claim in the appellate brief filed by Lomma's lawyers in their attempt to reverse the civil trial verdict.

"Crane operators often disable or override safety devices because . . . they trigger false alarms that interrupt and slow down work [my italics]," they wrote.

The jury *never* heard that assertion during the civil trial.

If there *was* a legitimate reason to turn off the crane's safeties, someone on the Sorbara crew might have done so. And if the safeties were disabled, Don *could* have inadvertently mishandled the crane.

Why didn't Fuerth make this argument? It would have been powerful, particularly since it squares with the plaintiffs' attorneys' own portrait of the construction industry as one in which speed trumps safety.

What's more, I remembered, it was an undisputed fact that the Ninety-First Street project was behind schedule, so it wouldn't have been surprising if the contractor or subcontractors had encouraged their workers, including the crane operators, to work faster.

September 14, 2017

The appellate court's decision in the case of Leo et al. v. Lomma et al. finally came in two days ago. It confirmed that Lomma, not Leo, caused the accident.

At first I thought, if this vaunted panel has definitively concluded that Lomma caused the collapse, who am I to question it? (And yes, it was not lost on me that the appellate judges were affording my jury's decision more respect than I was.)

But when I discovered that these five judges had made a couple of significant factual mistakes, I got my mojo back. They know the law behind this case better than I do, I thought; but I know the facts behind this case equally well, if not better.

* * *

When Bob got home from work, I showed him the decision. "The court lowered the damages *a lot*," Bob exclaimed. "From fifty-six million to nineteen million for Ramadan, and from forty million to sixteen million for Don."

"Indeed. And now that I believe our jury punished Lomma too harshly, I'm glad they reduced them," I replied. "But guess what? We jurors weren't the only ones who made errors. The appellate judges did, too. And if they hadn't made these mistakes, they might have lowered the damages even further."

"Are you sure they made errors? That's a serious claim."

"I'm sure. I read the decision several times, and I also carefully compared it with the trial's transcript. Let me show you."

I transformed our kitchen table into a judge's bench once again.

"Look at this line," I began. " 'The EMT reported Mr. Leo as alive and conscious approximately *seven minutes* [my italics] after the accident.' I don't know where on earth they found this statement. I checked the transcript several times: It's not there.

"In fact, the fire chief who coordinated the emergency response to the accident testified that when his team got to the site, Don had 'obvious mortal injuries,' " I continued. "This is why they focused all their efforts on rescuing Ramadan, who was still alive.

"In any case, the misbelief that Don was alive for seven minutes after the first responders arrived means the judges thought Don survived much longer than he actually did."

* * *

"There's more," I said. "Look at this part of the appellate court's decision."

" 'Lomma was aware that RTR [the Chinese company] stated in an email that it did not have confidence in its ability to weld the replacement component . . . '," Bob read aloud.

Wrong. Karten, one of the lawyers for the Kurtaj estate, confirmed that Lomma had *not* seen this email before the accident. The judges might have lowered *both* plaintiffs' damages even more if they hadn't gotten this wrong as well.

"Who knows? They might actually have decided that Lomma wasn't proven liable, and ordered a new trial."

TWELVE

STRAIGHT TALK FROM A DEFENDANT AND A LAWYER

July 23, 2018

"There's *no way* he'll meet with you," O'Neill, the attorney for Selvi Sinanovic (Ramadan's widow), replied when I told him I had requested an interview with Lomma.[5]

I proved O'Neill wrong.

About a month after I contacted Lomma, I heard from his in-house attorney, Chris Eriksen. He said Lomma was willing to be interviewed as long as I was open to hearing his no-holds-barred version of the Ninety-First Street accident. No problem, I thought: By agreeing to *listen* to Lomma, I wasn't agreeing to *believe* him. It would be a fair exchange for any new information Lomma might deliver.

---

5 My interview requests with the following trial participants were ignored or denied: Judge Mendez, Ms. Panzella, Ms. Karten, Mr. Fuerth, Ms. Williams, Mrs. Leo, Ms. Belcastro, and Ms. Sinanovic. I regret that I was unable to include their perspectives.

* * *

Our meeting was at one o'clock this afternoon at J.F. Lomma's New Jersey headquarters. I had expected a grim, gray edifice, in keeping with the industrial neighborhood in which it's located. Instead, I found an oasis of greenery: well-tended trees, a manicured lawn with a flagpole topped by the U.S. and New Jersey state flags, as well as a black-and-yellow "Lomma" banner, and neat shrubbery in front of a red-brick office building.

A woman with a full-blown smile greeted me, assuaging somewhat my nervousness, and led me down a hallway whose walls were lined with photos of cranes of various sizes and shapes, all sporting the Lomma logo. When I entered the big man's office, Lomma, along with Eriksen and an employee named Jimmy Upton, awaited.

Would this three-headed monster lay into me, the woman who cost their company millions of dollars, I wondered?

To my relief, they offered me a sealed (that is, poison-proof) bottle of water, and a chair (rather than a rack).

The "Lomma-landers," as I've nicknamed them, asked if they could make their presentation first, and I ceded the floor. Before I focused my attention on their pitch, I was distracted by my first ever close-up look at Lomma. His glasses, it turns out, are tinted for an innocent reason: He's cross-eyed.

The Lomma-landers began with an overview of the theory proposed by James Wiethorn, the accident reconstructionist who had been precluded in our trial. (I pretended to be unfamiliar with Wiethorn's argument, which I'd already learned about from my review of the criminal trial transcript.) "When I first approached Wiethorn," Lomma claimed, "he warned me that if he found that I was at fault, he would tell me so outright. I hired him anyway.

"Before I saw Wiethorn's analysis," Lomma continued, "I actually thought the weld *had* caused the accident. But afterwards, I was convinced that operator error was the culprit. Wiethorn really knows his stuff. Unlike the plaintiffs' expert, who had analyzed just one crane collapse before this one, Wiethorn had worked on eight hundred crane accident cases."

* * *

Lomma's cache of self-redemptive tools included a few digs at Don Leo. "I got a copy of Leo's application for a crane operator's license," Lomma said, "and he listed work experience he didn't have." How on earth would Lomma know that? I wondered. Did he contact the employers Don listed to verify whether or not he had worked there?

"Leo had never even operated a Kodiak crane before," Lomma continued. (This had been pointed out by Williams, Fuerth's associate, during the trial, but I didn't grasp its significance at the time.) "You see, because it runs so fast, a Kodiak requires particular expertise to operate," Lomma claimed. "Essentially, Leo was training on the streets of New York."

* * *

At this point, I was expecting Lomma to mention two further pieces of evidence that reflected poorly on Don, but had not been revealed during the trial. (I had found them in some of the case's supporting documents.) Surprisingly, Lomma kept mum. But I will divulge them now.

One: Don's postmortem toxicology report contained a startling finding—the presence of marijuana in his body. At first, I thought, does this mean Don was high on the morning of the accident? That would have blown the plaintiffs' case out of the water. The report's next sentence reassured me: "There were traces of marijuana in his bile and urine, but *not* in his blood," which means Don was *not* under the influence while operating the crane. (Apparently, blood indicates current use, while bile and urine indicate past use.)

Still, this new truth had given me pause. Even if Don wasn't under the influence on the morning of the accident, might he have been high on the job on previous occasions? I wondered. And if Don had had a urine test that morning, he would have failed. I assume he would have been severely reprimanded: He might possibly have had his crane operator's license suspended, or even revoked. No matter what, this new information made me question Don's overall judgment.

It also strengthened a belief I'd already begun to entertain more seriously: that, assuming the safeties had been disabled (which I now know is a distinct possibility, since there *is* a valid reason to do so), Don *could* have made mistakes on the morning of the accident.

Two: Don had a criminal record. In 1998, he was arrested for assault and battery, and he pled guilty to trespassing. Of course, this had nothing to do with Don's ability to operate a crane, so initially I thought this finding was irrelevant. However, the City's Department of Buildings considers it pertinent: According to current regulations, you can't get a crane operator's license if you have a criminal record.

What's more, this newly discovered fact marred ever so slightly Don's good-guy image, a portrayal that had unquestionably biased the jury in his favor.

* * *

"What was the criminal trial like for you?" I asked Lomma after his team had finished presenting their side of the story.

"You know, I could have taken a guilty plea and avoided the whole thing," he replied. "The D.A. would have waived prison time. But I refused, because I knew I was innocent."

"Mr. Lomma was very brave," interrupted Eriksen. "Most people would have taken the plea."

Brave, or arrogant, I thought.

"My criminal defense lawyers also did a great job," Lomma added.

"Speaking of lawyers, what did you think of your attorneys in the civil trial?" I asked.

"My insurance company chose Fuerth's firm," Lomma replied lukewarmly. "He did the best he could."

"Fuerth should have humanized you more," I opined. (During our interview, Lomma struck me as somewhat dull and humorless, but not villainous.) Lomma shrugged defensively, and I realized I'd insulted him by suggesting that he needed humanizing.

"Glenn *did* make one error," Lomma told me. "After the judge prevented Wiethorn, the accident reconstructionist, from testifying, Glenn knew things looked bad, and he considered settling with the plaintiffs."

Eriksen jumped in again. "There was *no* legitimate reason for precluding Wiethorn. Judge Mendez is not qualified. He doesn't know the law."

"Anyway," Lomma continued, "Glenn thought that the plaintiffs were still asking for too much money, so he decided to move forward with the trial. 'If we lose, the damages will total less than ten million dollars,' Glenn told me, 'so I think we should go ahead.' "

Given that our jury ended up awarding almost ninety-six million, I thought, that was a big mistake indeed. (Granted, the appellate judges lowered our damages to thirty-five million, but that's still twenty-five million more than Fuerth had anticipated.)

"What did you think about the amounts we awarded?" I mustered all my courage to ask Lomma.

"When the first verdict came in at forty-eight million, for compensatory damages," Lomma replied, "we were stunned. When the second verdict, for punitive damages, doubled the award to almost ninety-six million, we were flabbergasted. How did you guys come up with such big numbers?"

I breathed deeply, then summarized our deliberative process. To my surprise, Lomma took my explanation in stride.

* * *

"In the end, I lost," concluded Lomma. "I've got to move on. I'm the only one who gets hurt if I walk around with a chip on my shoulder.

"I'm in no position to retire," added Lomma, now seventy-three. "I sold all my real estate to pay the damages [Lomma's insurance didn't cover everything], but I still have to earn enough money to pay back what I borrowed to end the bankruptcy. [When Lomma filed his appeal, he also filed for bankruptcy, which allowed him to avoid paying the plaintiffs until after the appeal was decided.] Luckily, most businesses—except Sorbara—are still willing to work with me."

Upton finally spoke up. "Jimmy has so many friends in the industry. They've all told me not many people could have endured what he went through." Upton then showed me a press release announcing the "Golden Achievement Award" Lomma received, *during* the civil trial, from the Specialized Carriers and Rigging Association, a trade organization that counts several crane owners among its members.

The release listed Lomma's many accomplishments, including the fact that his cranes were dispatched posthaste to Ground Zero. (Free of charge, I wondered cynically?) The statement ended with the following: "To the core, James Lomma is compassionate. If you ask his competitors to describe him, they say he's a man of his word. He's got integrity, and he operates with a firm adherence to a strong ethical and moral code."

I wasn't buying this group's glowing portrait of Lomma; but, as I said before, I was no longer buying the plaintiffs' devil-incarnate portrait, either.

* * *

When I got ready to leave, Lomma pulled me aside. "You know, I feel very sorry for Mrs. Leo. She lost her son. My long-deceased mother would be angry with me for speaking ill of a dead man.

"I actually met Don Leo a few times," Lomma added. "In fact, I took my crane operator's test along with him. I even knew his father. He knew his son wasn't qualified, but he pushed him into the union so he could get a high-paying job as a tower crane operator.[6] I think Don's dad felt bad, that it was *his* fault that his son died. That's why

---

6 Later I interviewed a tower crane operator with no connection to the Ninety-First Street accident who corroborated Lomma's opinion. "Don Leo was way too young to operate a tower crane," he told me. "His father must have pulled some strings to get him that job." This operator also confirmed that there are times when crane crews *do* disable the safety devices.

he died three years after the accident—he drank himself to death.[7]"

These claims made me dizzy. Was there *any* truth to *any* of them, I wondered?

August 30

This afternoon, I visited Michael O'Neill, the attorney for Ramadan Kurtaj's widow, in his downtown Manhattan office. O'Neill's "firm" includes just him and his office-manager wife, Natasha Hasib. The rooms were sparsely and humbly furnished. "I'd like to renovate," Natasha told me. "But my husband doesn't want to spend the money." Even though he has plenty of it now, I thought.

* * *

"Please, call me Mike," O'Neill said as I took a seat across from him at his enormous desk, piled so high with paperwork that I could barely see or hear him. "So, what do you want to know?"

"First of all, I was wondering if you, Karten, and Panzella tried to settle the case before going to trial," I began.

"Yes, absolutely," Mike replied. "But there were a couple of stumbling blocks. First, there were so many defendants—"

"Tell me about it," I interrupted.

---

7 Lomma died nine months after our interview. (As of 2021, his businesses are still active.)

"Believe it or not, there were *way* more when the case began. Anyway, all of them wanted the other defendants to pay. Plus the insurance companies were fighting one another, so no single party was willing to cough up much money.

"The defendants are likely kicking themselves now," Mike added.

"Because they submitted themselves to the hassle of a year-long trial?" I asked.

"Well, there's that," Mike chuckled. "Also, we would have settled for a lot less money than we ended up getting."

"Really?"

"Yep. That's because, for one thing, the value of Don Leo's noneconomic damages was minimal, since he died almost instantly."

Whoa. Did Mike just baldly refute Panzella's claim that Don had survived up to twenty-seven minutes, a claim that even the appellate judges seemed to have believed?

"After the accident, Ramadan remained conscious for forty-five minutes to a couple of hours," Mike continued. Not *four* hours, as he and Karten had claimed, and the appellate judges had concluded. "So, compared with awards for pre-impact fear and post-impact pain and suffering with similar time frames, Don's noneconomic damages were worth one to two million dollars, and Ramadan's were worth three to four million."

There it was: a forthright appraisal of the value of the decedents' noneconomic damages. When I compared this three to four million with the thirty-five million Karten had requested for Ramadan in her closing statement, I felt queasy.

How could Mike, in good conscience, justify this discrepancy? Afraid to annoy my subject and possibly end the interview prematurely, I didn't ask. Would he have tried to defend it by claiming it was his duty to get as much money as possible for his client, even if it was more than deserved?

The expected economic damages in the case were also minimal, Mike explained. "See, Don didn't support anyone," he stated unequivocally, blowing another of Panzella's claims—that Don supported and would have continued to support his mother—out of the water. "And Selvi's inheritance was in dispute because of the separation and her out-of-wedlock child."

"And the fact that theirs was a marriage of convenience," I added.

"No, they really did love each other," Mike insisted. I couldn't believe Mike *still* wouldn't let go of that claim, I thought.

* * *

When I asked Mike if he would have preferred to try the case on his own, unlinked to the Leo action or to Karten's client, he replied in the negative. "Bernadette and Sue fought really hard. They took these wrongs very personally. They have a real sense of justice. Particularly when it came to the decision to ask for punitive damages. If you picked two other lawyers at random, they probably would have said, 'It's really hard to get punitive damages.

Let's not bother. Let's just get a few million and move on.' These two didn't do that."

Reading between the lines, I got the sense that Mike was indebted to Bernadette and Sue for helping him earn the most money in his career from one single case.

"How did you end up representing Selvi, anyway?" I asked Mike.

"It was happenstance. Selvi called a phone number for legal services that she'd seen in a TV commercial, and her case was randomly assigned to me."

I didn't tell Mike that I'd discovered (in a supporting document that I'd found on the court's website) the *real* reason behind that phone call. Jev Sinanaj, the representative for Ramadan's parents, had told a surrogate's court judge that Ramadan was *not* married. (Jev was Karten's receptionist when Ramadan died, which is how Karten got the case.[8]) When Selvi found out about this fraudulent representation—which would have cut her out of her inheritance—she realized she had to find an attorney of her own.

"Selvi got lucky," Mike opined. "There are a lot of substandard personal injury lawyers out there."

I nodded.

"Of course, I ended up getting lucky, too," Mike added.

* * *

---

8 Panzella was hired by Don Leo's father, *not* Maria Leo. Panzella had represented Don Leo's father in a matter related to his job as a firefighter. Panzella was also a friend of his girlfriend.

"Let's talk about the elephant in the room: the length of the case," I announced abruptly.

"Okay. I know it was hard on the jury," Mike replied. "Bernadette, Sue, and I are eternally grateful to all of you."

"Imagine if, after a whole year, we had found for the defendants."

"That would have been a nightmare for us. Fuerth suffered the stigma of losing, but at least he still got paid for his time."

"Whose fault was it that the trial was so long?" I asked.

"Well, it *was* a complicated case, with two plaintiffs and several defendants," Mike replied. "Plus, we had additional claims against some of the defendants that the jury never knew about."

"Really?"

"You see, in New York City, there's something called the 'Scaffold Law,' " Mike explained. "This statute holds owners, developers, and contractors strictly liable for any gravity-related casualties on a construction site, no matter who's at fault. [In our case, this law applied *only* to the landowner, the developers, and the general contractor, DeMatteis; it did *not* apply to subcontractor Sorbara, Lomma and his companies, or Brady Marine.] We settled these claims before your verdict. But, of course, we still had the negligence claims, the ones you jurors *did* have to decide."

In effect, some of the defendants were charged twice— under the Scaffold Law *and* through negligence claims—for the same casualties. Seemed unfair to me, the equivalent of double jeopardy in a criminal case.

"Okay. But anyway, couldn't the judge have shortened the trial? He let all the lawyers, particularly Panzella, go on and on forever."

"Yeah, of course he could have. But Mendez didn't want to create the argument that somebody didn't get to present their case sufficiently. Besides, the job of the judge is not to shape the case. He can say what *can* and *cannot* be asked, but not what *should* and *shouldn't* be asked."

"Did you ever get nervous that, because of the length of the trial, you'd lose one too many jurors?"

"Sure. But once you were down to seven, I sensed a determination that you'd be there forever, if it came down to it."

"You're right about that. We weren't about to give up after all the sweat and tears we'd poured into the proceeding."

"I was very happy to leave the case in your hands. Obviously, we lawyers were watching you all very carefully. We were always speculating about what you were thinking. You, Cynthia, were pretty easy to read. I bet you don't play poker."

"I've played a couple of times, but I'm really bad at it," I admitted with a laugh.

"That was great! There's nothing worse for a lawyer than a stone-faced juror."

* * *

When we wrapped up the interview, Mike told me that he, Sue, and Bernadette were planning a dinner to honor the jury. "Keep an eye out for the invitation!"

It came a few days later, as did a quirky newsletter O'Neill sends to clients and "friends of the firm," of which, I guess, I'm now one. Labeled "So Much Fun Inside It Should Be Illegal—But I'm a Lawyer, So It's Okay," it included an article about a Roman god; a piece on the "lunacy of the electoral college"; a reader contest about math and the law; and two back-page photos.

One was of Mike standing next to a ceiling-high stack of documents related to the Lomma case. Now that it's over, I can picture his Cheshire-cat grin when he knocks it down.

THIRTEEN

FINAL ANSWER?

Why did a crane fall out of the sky above New York City on May 30, 2008?

I'll never really know.

But given the facts I've uncovered since the civil trial ended, I have to entertain the possibility that the accident may have had not *one*, but *two* causes.

Don Leo *could* have mishandled the crane to such an extent that the flawed weld failed.

Why wasn't the possibility of two causes *ever* considered in this decade-long legal odyssey?

Because, if true, it would mean that *both* sides were at fault. Both sides would be losers. And nobody, particularly lawyers, likes to lose.

* * *

Perhaps the defense attorney in the movie *A Civil Action* was right when he declared, "The courtroom is *not* the place to look for the truth."

FOURTEEN

CODA

Today was Election Day, and I felt a tinge of melancholy as I headed to my polling site to cast my ballot.

I voted in the very school that was built in conjunction with the condominium for which Donald Christopher Leo and Ramadan Kurtaj gave their lives. (Sadly, I know of one other death associated with this building: One my neighbors committed suicide by jumping off its roof.) Called "The Azure," the condominium's latest marketing slogan is, ironically, "The Color of Life."

Before I left, I stopped by the memorial to Don and Ramadan that one of the school's students suggested be hung in a hallway outside the library. Topped by photos of each man, it reads:

On Friday, May 30, 2008, a crane collapsed on the corner of Ninety-First Street and First Avenue, resulting in the deaths of Donald Leo and Ramadan Kurtaj, two construction workers building East Side Middle School and the adjoining apartments.

Donald Leo wanted to be a crane operator like his father since he was a young boy. He enjoyed playing sports, a passion he shared with the children in his neighborhood, who welcomed the chance to play wiffle ball with him. Donald was raised on Staten Island and more recently resided in New Jersey with his fiancée, Janine Belcastro. Donald Leo was thirty years old.

Ramadan Kurtaj arrived in the United States two years ago from Kosovo, where he had fought as a soldier in the conflict in the Balkans. Mr. Kurtaj worked in construction to help support his family, including his parents in Kosovo. Ramadan Kurtaj was twenty-seven [sic] years old.

It was a modest testimonial that captured a simple truth. Possibly the only truth behind this accident that can ever be known with one hundred percent certainty. That the quest of two young men—to live, each in his own way, the American dream—was cruelly dashed.

NOTE

This is a nonfiction book in which everything I describe is factually true.

I did, however, make the following alterations for clarity and narrative purposes.

In the Prologue, I imagined some details of Don Leo's and Ramadan Kurtaj's pre-accident mornings.

In Part One, I edited (sometimes heavily, since courtroom discourse can be ponderous), and changed the order of, some of the quotes from the trial's transcript; I rearranged the sequence of witnesses, and excluded many of them; I changed the dates of some of the testimony and other events that took place inside the courtroom and the jury room; and I recreated from memory the dialogue among the jurors, sometimes combining parts of separate conversations into one.

In Part Two, I switched the order of, and changed the dates of, my interviews with Mr. Lomma and Mr. O'Neill.

ACKNOWLEDGMENTS

Most book acknowledgments end with thanks for supportive spouses. But mine gets first billing.

My husband, Bob, lent me his legal expertise in countless ways. (If I'd married a doctor, I don't know if I'd have been able to write this book.) He answered my many questions about the law; he helped me navigate the New York County Supreme Court's website, plus other impenetrable legal resources; and he even snuck me into the New York City Bar Association's library.

Bob also lent me his writing and editing expertise. He recognized the story potential behind my jury duty experience and encouraged me to write this book; he read and edited several iterations; and he provided feedback on the tens of titles I proposed.

Most importantly, Bob lent me his patience. He never complained when I'd make him wait until late at night to sit down to dinner together because I needed "five more minutes" to finish a paragraph; he didn't get angry when I argued with him about a matter of law that I was sure I had right and he had wrong (even though *he's* the lawyer, not me); and he tolerated my repeated requests to explain a legal term just "one last time."

I was lucky to have had the help of two great editors, Paula Derrow and Jason O'Toole, who advised me wisely and kindly. I'm also grateful to a friend from college, lawyer and writer Susan Beck, who read the manuscript and gave me terrific suggestions.

Eleven thank-yous are due to eleven strangers who became eleven jurors who became eleven friends. As Tony put it, "We are bonded for life." Special thanks to Alison Colby, who graciously permitted me to include some of her superb sketches in this book.

Several of the civil trial lawyers helped me enormously. One of the defense attorneys, who shall remain nameless because he/she might get in trouble with the court reporters, saved me thousands of dollars by sharing the civil and criminal trial transcripts with me free of charge. This same lawyer spared me many hours of frustration by spending an afternoon explaining documents to me.

Susan Karten and Craig Snyder, the lawyers for Ramadan Kurtaj's parents, kept me abreast of important post–civil trial proceedings. Bernadette Panzella, who represented the Leo estate, gave me a lot of behind-the-scenes information. Many thanks are due to Michael O'Neill, Selvi Sinanovic's attorney, who answered my interview questions patiently and entertainingly.

Other interviewees who deserve my thanks: the now-deceased James Lomma, as well as his employees, Chris Eriksen and Jimmy Upton, who treated me politely and respectfully; and Daniel Mooney, a crane operator who granted an interview to a total stranger.

Finally, thank you to my children, James and Jules, for supporting my endeavor, for answering my countless word-processing questions, and for putting up with my peculiar obsession with cranes.

ABOUT THE AUTHOR

Cynthia M. Pigott is a former magazine editor and writer. *Diary of a Mad Juror* is her first book.

Made in United States
Orlando, FL
30 November 2021

10982014R00150